Earth Is Overpopulated Now

Earth Is Overpopulated Now

David E. Christensen, PhD

iUniverse, Inc.
New York Lincoln Shanghai

Earth Is Overpopulated Now

iUniverse books may be ordered through booksellers or by contacting:

iUniverse
2021 Pine Lake Road, Suite 100
Lincoln, NE 68512
www.iuniverse.com
1-800-Authors (1-800-288-4677)

The views expressed in this work are solely those of the author and do not necessarily reflect the views of the publisher, and the publisher (as is its policy with all works of a political nature) hereby disclaims any responsibility for them.

ISBN-13: 978-0-595-42427-6 (pbk)
ISBN-13: 978-0-595-86762-2 (ebk)
ISBN-10: 0-595-42427-9 (pbk)
ISBN-10: 0-595-86762-6 (ebk)

Printed in the United States of America

DEDICATION

"EARTH IS OVERPOPULATED NOW" is dedicated to my six grandchildren, Laura, Brian, Tory, Cassie, Nicole and Megan, and also to the twenty-one other children and young adults for whom I am a "great uncle".

A Special Message to My Grandchildren—and to All Grandchildren:

The future is yours and that is what this book is all about.

I have four hopes for the time—in a very few years—when you take over to "run the world":

> I hope the world we oldsters leave you will have abandoned the wasteful and long outdated use of war to settle issues between groups of grownups.
> I hope the world's population will be stable and then declining.
> I hope a Limited Global Government will have been established and be working well.
> I hope the world will be approaching a sustainable balance between the Earth's offerings and what all living things, including humans, take from the Earth.

If these important "hopes" have not been accomplished by the time the world "is yours", please work hard to help make them happen. The sooner the better!

I wish each of you a long and healthy life filled with love, satisfying work and happiness—in a world of challenge, striving for "peace and goodwill among the human family".

Lovingly,
Grandpa and Great Uncle Dave
November 2006

Contents

PREFACE

My *Healing the World*, published in 2005, and this book, *Earth is Overpopulated Now*, present issues and concerns that have been on the mind of this retired geography professor and many others for years. After decades of teaching about what is happening to our Earth home and how we have been wasting people and the Earth's treasure, especially in wars, I retired in 1984, and since then other problems have become as pressing as the war and energy problems.

I was moved to write these two books in part because in my judgment the United States' current administration in Washington and the Congress are ignoring the Constitution, are steadily weakening our middle class—the backbone of any democracy, and are not addressing the critical issues. The second Bush administration has ignored global warming and speeded the deterioration of the environment. Their profit and oil-oriented foreign policy and illegal preemptive war against Iraq have made the United States an international pariah, squandering the goodwill our country engendered among the nations for generations.

As I explain in the Introduction to this book, because of comments I received from those who read *Healing the World*, I recognized the need for a follow-up book. Outlines and drafts of a few parts of *Earth is Overpopulated Now* were written in early 2005 but most of it was written from January through July 2006, with some tinkering and updating until November 2006.

I am very thankful to my family and friends who encouraged me to pursue this follow-up book project. Without their support it might not have been done. Perhaps they are happy to see their Dad, brother or friend keeping busy, but especially on something they agree is very important!

A few friends were kind enough to read an early draft of this volume and offer major and minor suggestions, all of which are deeply appreciated and most of which have been adopted. Readers of an early draft were David Gobert, Bill Sasso, and Jack Stewart, a retired French professor, a Unitarian-Universalist minister, and a farmer/philosopher.

I also appreciate the help I received from the staff of iUniverse at all stages in my self-publishing this book and my earlier book.

David E. Christensen
November 2006

INTRODUCTION

The population of the world was about 2 billion when I was born in 1921, and it is 6.5 billion this year (2006). With about 120 million now being added each year, the population of the world is expected to reach 7 billion by 2010. The population of the United States was 107 million in my birth year and 85 years later is 300 million (October 2006).

The Earth simply cannot provide adequately for such gains! We already are living beyond the Earth's ability to provide adequate food and other necessities for the present population. That is the basic message of this book and it will be bad news, especially for our children and grandchildren, if intelligent action is not begun now to face the ecological and other catastrophes that are on the way. If we do not face up to these converging catastrophes a Dark Age will be upon us.

Looking up "overpopulation" and "Zero Population Growth" on the Internet brings up the following two quotes: Paul Ehrlich (author of the 1968 bestseller, *The Population Bomb*) said,

"We shouldn't delude ourselves: the population explosion will come to an end before very long. The only remaining question is whether it will be halted through the humane method of birth control or by nature wiping out the surplus. We realize that religious and cultural opposition to birth control exists throughout the world, but we believe that people simply don't understand the choice that such opposition implies."

And Robert McNamara, former Secretary of Defense and President of the World Bank, was more specific in his prediction (probably in a May 1969 speech):

"Dire consequences would spread like an atomic cloud. Third world families would be driven to an unprecedented level of abortion and infanticide—particularly of female babies. Developing countries would be left with massive unemployment, hideously sprawling cities, woefully inadequate food supplies, ravaged environments and a frightening increase of absolute poverty, a term for living conditions so characterized by malnutrition, illiteracy and disease as to be beneath any reasonable definition of human decency."

These dire consequences about overpopulation were before us in the 1960s but little has happened. You might wonder why our leaders and the media are not informing us about over-population and the other crises. The answer is painfully clear: Government leaders in Washington and state capitols in the United States are beholden to the corporations that fill their campaign coffers and do not want to upset citizens whose votes are needed. Corporate CEOs do not want to upset their profit making operations; and the media is part of the corporate world. Also, for two hundred years new technologies have come along quite regularly which made it possible to support more and more people.

For decades there have been writers calling public attention to the ways in which the human family is not using the Earth's offerings wisely. Titles and key words in the titles of some of these books are "food", "land", "hunger", "soil", "survival", "limits", *The Population Bomb*, *The Population Explosion*, *Standing Room Only*, "overpopulation" and *The Long Emergency*. These and other books are listed in Appendix A.

Taken together, the words and titles noted above convey an ominous message relating to the Earth's "carrying capacity" for humans. It is the same message I am trying to present in these pages: a deep-seated concern about the future of the human family and our civilization, a concern that calls for immediate action by the *PEOPLE*.

The term "carrying capacity" usually refers to the number of livestock that can be supported on a given acreage of pasture. "Carrying capacity for humans" refers to the number of individuals who can be supported in a particular area (or on the Earth) *INDEFINITELY* with no ill effects to the natural environment. Carrying capacity for humans might be thought of in the form of a "People to Earth Equation". *What the human family takes from the Earth must not be more than the Earth can provide and renew on a continuing basis.*

Those who have written in the past and are writing now about these important topics are not "doomsayers" who have given up on the prospects of the great human experiment on the Earth. Of course not. You surely would want your neighbor to call 911 and alert you if your house was on fire! If these writers and I had no hope for the future of the human family on Earth we would not have bothered to write at all. We do have hope IF action will be taken soon on our message! We are appealing to the intelligence and compassion of the world's people! We have written to try to awaken those who can pull levers of power and to help educate the people to take action in time on the critical issues.

The writers mentioned, and others who have called public attention to the sad state of the world's "People-Earth Equation", were prophetic. In the 1930s the "Revolution of Rising Expectations" among the people in developing countries was acknowledged, and "human rights" were on the minds of thoughtful individuals and leaders. Even decades ago this non-violent "revolution" and interest in "human rights" were fueling unrest among the world's billions of poor and starving people, but the dangerous march toward the "overpopulation" of the Earth was not taken seriously until the 1960s, and since then only by a few (publicly).

There are many among us who brush off the idea of overpopulation in the belief that human ingenuity, as in the past, will come to the rescue, with new ways of providing whatever a growing world population needs. Just because the inventiveness of the human family in the past has led to new technologies to provide for a growing human family (aided by generous supplies of relatively cheap fossil fuels in our time) is no guarantee it will continue. There can be no assurance that new technologies will come along or be adopted in time to overcome the critical issues that are undermining the viability of the human family on Earth. We should not gamble the future of our species on hopes. We should plan for the future based *only* on knowledge, technologies and resources that are available to develop a sustainable system based on the Earth's offerings.

Despite the impressive advances that are part of the fabric of life for most people in North America, Europe, Japan, Australia and a few other places, most of our brothers and sisters on this planet do not share our advantages of education, health care, economic opportunity, freedom, and security. Very few advantages of modern progressive civilization are evident in the lives of most of the human family, and things are getting worse.

It is eminently clear that those in "developing countries" know very well about our more comfortable way of life and they understand that their deprivation is somehow related to our prosperity. The "Revolution of Rising Expectations" is fueling unrest that has turned some people to violence and terrorism in too many places. After all, by what right do we in the "Western World" of "rich" consumers and powerful corporations have to control and use most of the world's energy and mineral resources? What right do we have to intervene in and dominate "developing countries" with a new kind of "economic colonialism"?

Overpopulation and This Book. Deciding on a title for this book was a problem because the word "overpopulation" raises several issues. One is that it may engender in some people the notion of letting the sick, infirm, elderly and poor die off—a genocidal approach such as Scrooge suggested—so the survivors might have better lives. The overpopulation issue also raises the "hot button" birth control and abortion controversies that include differing beliefs as to when "personhood" begins and the sanctity of life.

My concern for these matters goes back decades, but the idea for this book came early in 2005 before *Healing the World* was published in late 2005. Part of my concern stems from my judgment as a geographer, revealed in the title, that even now our "human family" is too large for all members to achieve a way of life that approximates that of most citizens in the United States, Europe and a few other places on Earth.

But why should I write another book, especially since the first one—with its urgent message focusing on three crises facing the human family—did not light a fire of interest among the 100 plus members of Congress and other leaders to whom I sent a copy? Surely our leaders and parents with children and young people should be very concerned about the years ahead!

The three critical problems I focused on in *Healing the World* are: [1] The United States' militarized foreign policy is wasteful, futile, is driving us into bankruptcy, and is making us less secure. [2] Economic "globalization" is dominated by greedy multi-national corporations and is proceeding to the detriment of most people in "developing countries". And [3] we are in desperate need of a sustainable relationship between humans and the Earth and to overcome critical environmental problems, such as addiction to oil and global climate change ("global warming"). These critical issues are still there and solutions are becoming more urgent and difficult with each passing month. *Healing the World* also explained why I believe a Limited Global Government is the only way to deal with global issues such as these three.

Overpopulation, the overarching concern of this book, was mentioned only a few times in *Healing the World*. After reading that book several individuals asked me why I believe the world is already overpopulated, and I realize I did not present my reasons for believing so. And I also did not take up the logical follow-up question: "If the Earth is already overpopulated, is there anything that we, as caring humans, can do about the present 'surplus' and the billions more coming on?" That question has serious implications that must involve our Earth home, our beliefs and values, our religion, and our concerns and hopes for the future of the human family. Questions about these concerns, the Earth's basic resources, the Earth's "carrying capacity" for humans, and what we can and must do about it are the focus of this book.

Earth Is Overpopulated Now, like my 2005 book, was written for an "average world citizen", and particularly for United States citizens. It was *not* written for those who are convinced the human family is already too large for the Earth to provide a decent level of living for all. It was *not* written for those already convinced that a Limited Global Government, however it might be achieved, is the way toward solution of global issues. Furthermore, if you already are convinced that our energy crisis is real and, perhaps by Al Gore's movie and book (*An Inconvenient Truth*), that global warming is happening, you still will find much to think about in this book.

But if you *are* already convinced of these critical converging realities, my questions then would be, "What are you doing about it?" "What actions have you taken?"

Nobel Laureate Wole Soyinka, author of *Climate of Fear,* observed that for all the power and technological advances of our country, most Americans think they know enough about the world, when in fact they do not. Our educational system, generally weak in geography and science instruction, has not helped Americans to be well informed about the Earth's natural systems and about "how the world works" for us and our billions of neighbors on this planet. The American public's general ignorance about world geography makes them particularly gullible to propaganda and simplistic military "solutions" to important foreign policy issues.

Our educational system and our media do not help us learn to ask important questions, to sift fact from hype and fiction, or to reason carefully. Our educational system steers clear of controversial issues and emphasizes factual, testable information. Our corporate owned media is far more interested in running advertisements, profit-making and pleasing shareholders than informing an electorate about critical issues, so vital to a democracy. As for our legislative "leaders", many are themselves ignorant of the real world issues and are more concerned about party loyalty and finding money for reelection campaigns than they are about dealing realistically and fairly about important issues that must be faced "for the general welfare" and the "common good".

There is a huge problem to get the attention of "The People" in the United States. Democracy is predicated on the principle of an informed citizenry in voting booths making free and responsible choices on issues of importance to them. If they must vote based on inadequate, misleading or false information, it is a sham democracy and voting choices will be flawed and will not be in the real interest of most citizens.

Further, people are busy every day with their own personal problems. These days many are unemployed by corporate downsizing and have lost health care and even pension commitments. Many family members are being forced to juggle two or more jobs. It is no surprise that many have little inclination or time to keep up with national or world issues. At election time citizens are wooed for their votes and are likely to get only sound bites that don't inform, dirty negative campaigning, outright lies and skewed information. Even then a cloud hangs over the voting process as to whether their votes will be counted honestly. There are reasons behind the low voter turnout in the U.S. (I make several suggestions for election reform in the Epilogue.)

It is the writer's hope that, with the knowledge and perspectives shared, readers will work at being more informed citizens and act on their concerns. I hope that informed citizens in democracies everywhere will elect those who will make intelligent decisions for improving the well being, not only of those within their countries, but because we are now so interdependent, for the entire human family and our Earth home. I hope especially that many young people will read this and other books and articles on the overpopulation and other critical issues and become motivated and mobilized to take action.

World Encompassing Ecological and Other Studies. The work of decades is summarized in Paul and Anne Ehrlich's 1990 *The Population Explosion.* This important book recounts the history of humans on Earth and paints a grim picture about how in our time humans are overwhelming the Earth. The Ehrlichs introduced the "I = PAT" formula, which relates a nation's Impact on the Earth to Population, Affluence and Technology. They asserted that the

Earth was already overpopulated in 1990, and they forecasted gloom if population is not reduced.

Since the 1970s Lester R. Brown and his associates at the World Watch Institute (now called the Earth Policy Institute) have analyzed and written persuasively about how humans are using and misusing their Earth home. Their findings are not encouraging. In their annual reports they focus on deterioration in all aspects of our "misuse". As examples, note these chapter sub-headings in Brown's 2005 book, *Plan B 2.0*: Falling Water Tables, Rivers Running Dry, Rising Temperatures and Its Effects, Shrinking Forests, Losing Soil, Deteriorating Rangelands, Advancing Deserts, Collapsing Fisheries, Disappearing Plants and Animals, Health Challenge Growing, Throwaway Economy in Trouble, and much more. *Plan B 2.0* goes on to discuss ways in which we can deal with the deterioration of each of these basic resources. A "must read and take action" book for all Americans.

Deriving from Brown's annual "State of the World" and "Plan B" studies is the Jerome C. Glenn and Theodore J. Gordon study, *State of the Future 2005*, presented in a 3500 page CD and an Executive Summary. The report was developed through the American Council for The U.N. University as part of the U.N. Millennium Project (next paragraphs). Glenn and Gordon's study makes recommendations on a variety of goals for the U.N. in this new century, including many suggestions for U.N. reform as well as targets to improve the lives of Earth's inhabitants.

The U.N. Millennium Project was a study effort commissioned by U.N. Secretary General Kofi Annan to set goals for resolving some of the world's most difficult human problems. The Advisory Commission completed the *Millennium Declaration* (MD) in 2000 and it was adopted in September 2005 by 147 heads of state. The MD was patterned after two of President Franklin Delano Roosevelt's "Four Freedoms": Freedom from Want and Freedom from Fear, but it has received very little media attention in the United States.

The *Millennium Declaration* involved the work of nearly 2000 scientists and creative people from dozens of countries. This detailed multi-part study analyzes many Earth-People issues and presents detailed challenges to all nations and people to take immediate action if we are to avert very difficult times in the near future for ourselves and our children. The MD presented 18 goals that were compressed into 8, and all were to be completed or well underway by 2015. One formidable goal among the 8 is to reduce world poverty by half by the year 2015. At least the entire Executive Summary [Excerpted in Appendix B] also should be "must" reading for concerned world citizens.

In 2000 and backed by the U.N., the *Millennium Ecosystem Assessment* is a forward-looking study about what life on our planet would be like in 2050, when U.N. projections suggest that the world's population will have increased to between 8.1 and 9.6 billions. A report on the Internet by Tracy Hukill informs us that this $24 million study, which involved more than 1,300 scientists in 95 countries over four years, hardly raised a ripple in the U.S. media when it was released in December 2005. The report presents four different scenarios of Earth's ecosystems and the consequences to the human family. The most discouraging is for us to continue the wasteful and careless ways we do things now; the most encouraging scenario informs us that if the human family is to survive and prosper we must make many changes in our eco-behavior and how we deal with each other [http://www.alternet.org.story/31222/].

These reports relate directly to the "People-Earth Equation", the balance that must be established between what the Earth can provide on a continuing basis and what humans (and all other living things) may use on a sustainable (forever) basis. The importance of these reports for the future of mankind is enormous.

As Hukill said, "The (*Millennium Ecosystem Assessment*) report's basic premise is that healthy ecosystems provide humans with a range of 'services'—things like food, clean water, clean air, buffers from natural disasters and even spiritual renewal. To the extent that these 'ecosystem services' are degraded, so is the quality of human life."

Hukill reports further that Walt Reid, who directed the study and teaches at Stanford, "concluded that 60 percent of the planet's ecosystem services are being run down or used up faster than they can replenish themselves", and that "without serious behavior modification, we're headed for a bad run."

Looking at these recent comprehensive studies that focus on the "People-Earth Equation", one cannot help but be encouraged on the one hand, but discouraged on the other. I am encouraged because these excellent and thought-provoking studies present hard data on what is happening. I am discouraged because they are largely ignored by the media and therefore do not engage the interest or concern of large numbers of United States citizens and our fellow world citizens. To protect profits or to avoid facing up to difficult issues, the media and public discourse on the one hand tend to "mountainize" the trivial and, on the other hand, to ignore or trivialize problems and issues that truly *are* of "mountainous" concern for the public and our "civilization".

About "Geography" and this Geographer. Geography is a unique discipline that has "one foot" in the physical sciences and the "other foot" in the social sciences. Geographers are deeply and equally concerned with how elements of the social and cultural environment and elements of the physical environment interact and affect the well being of people living in a particular place. With this approach geography is a remarkable "bridging" discipline and can provide insight into complex problems as well as insight into both the already introduced "People-Earth Equation" and the "People-People Equation", which concerns how people deal with each other in the world.

For years I would ask my students to look out the classroom window. I would then ask them what they see, and their answers would be trees, people, other buildings, etc. Then I'd ask if they see any "chemistry", "geology", "mathematics", "sociology", "literature", or even "geography" out there, and the answers were blurry. They said they could see chemistry in action; they could see evidence of human action; they knew that geology was under the ground everywhere. They knew they could measure or count or write about many things they saw. But separate disciplines were not there. The point is that all of those subjects—in an intermingled way—are included in the holistic functioning and reality of what is all around us. This is the real world, and each of the many subject disciplines humans invented focuses on a facet of that reality.

E. O. Wilson was getting at this unity of everything in his book, *Consilience*. Except for history and geography, rarely are connections made with other disciplines to try to understand the functioning whole. Just as geography attempts to make connections among many physical and social realities on the Earth's surface, history attempts to understand and make connections of the many past realities over time. Unfortunately "history is written by the winners" and as it is taught and researched, history focuses more on wars and leaders than problems of the people.

It was geography's eclectic nature, its search for holistic understandings about the world today and my fascination with maps that attracted me to the discipline in 1939. As a new Assistant Professor of Geography at Florida State University in Tallahassee in 1948 I became familiar with two introductory textbooks that were written by FSU Professors Henry F. Becker and Harry

Brubaker. These textbooks were built around six "bridging" questions. The answers to these questions help one understand how well a group of people or a nation is getting along in a particular area and how improvements might be made. The six questions, listed below, are still relevant to basic geography:

1. What specific elements of the natural environment have favored support of people, and what elements of the natural environment have limited economic activity?

2. How are people using the NATURAL RESOURCES of their region? And who is being advantaged or disadvantaged by that development?

3. What are the HUMAN RESOURCES of the region or nation? "Human resources" include the mental and physical qualities of people living in a particular place, including health, strength, level of education, ability to reproduce more humans, as well as their ability to feel emotions.

4. How successful is the region/nation in the number of people supported and the quality of their lives (measured in several ways) and the amount of wealth created?

5. What internal and external CULTURAL RESOURCES have favored progress and success? Are there cultural elements that have retarded progress and success? "Cultural resources" include institutions of all kinds as well as religious beliefs and even attitudes that encourage or discourage change and innovation.

6. And what are the major cultural and other problems that must be solved to achieve a more successful way of life for the people of the region/nation?

A further explanation is needed about resources since sub-classifications of Natural Resources especially are of particular concern to humans in the "Earth-People Equation".

The term NATURAL RESOURCES refers to anything in nature for which humans have found a use. Obviously, people in different places will have differing concepts about what in their environment is useful and what is not, based on their cumulative cultural experience. There also are three sub-categories of Natural Resources: 1. The Earth's supply of some natural resources for practical purposes may be considered Unlimited (solar power, salt water, air, sand, rocks and minerals of various kinds, wind, geothermal heat, etc.). Not all of these are equally available everywhere in the same condition. In the case of the atmosphere, rivers, lakes and oceans, local or widespread pollution might compromise their usability.

The unlimited energy from the sun, which will continue for several billion more years, demands special comment. Even though the sun is not a large star, its output of energy is so enormous it is difficult to comprehend. The Earth intercepts only about one six-trillionth of the sun's total energy output, which reaches us as a beam of light. Infinitesimal as is this portion of the sun's output, this micro-fraction of the sun's energy is the basis of all life and activity on Earth.

2. Exhaustible resources or Non-Renewable natural resources (coal, petroleum, natural gas, etc.) are those that, no matter how carefully they are used, will be depleted by using them. These energy resources may be being made in the Earth even now, but if so it would be at rates so slow as to provide no basis for countering their depletion. The best humans can do with "exhaustible resources" is to be as efficient as possible during their "one time use".

Common metals like aluminum, iron, steel, copper and others are made from ores in nature that are limited in quantity. However, once refined they are Reusable IF humans collect and recycle them.

3. In a very real sense, Renewable natural resources (soil, grassland, forests, fisheries, fresh water, and most other living things) are the most important of all natural resources for supporting all living forms. These are resources on which the human family (and all creatures) depend daily and directly for food, fiber, water, and some energy and construction needs. These must support the present and the future of all living things on the Earth. Depending on the manner in which humans use these, they can be renewed and maintained by natural processes and human actions OR be depleted. The key point is that they are "renewable" only if they are not mismanaged or overused.

However, renewability is a relative matter. For some species of trees it takes hundreds of years to grow to be of use to mankind. "Renewability" in that time frame would have little practicality to the average farmer or forest manager. Some rapid growing trees are grown for paper and poles and can be harvested in a decade or two, so these *can* be dealt with as a crop and a "renewable resource". Also of great significance are the many non-economic functions of forests to stabilize the ground and control the rate of runoff from hills and mountains.

Soil is also listed as a renewable natural resource, but again it is a relative matter. It takes hundreds of years for natural processes to develop an inch of soil.

Thus for practical purposes our soil has to be managed very carefully at all times so it will not be depleted. Its renewability is so slow that, for our survival, we should not let anyone mismanage this very important resource. Raising one or two crops on the same land over and over also is a problem in agriculture because fertilizers do not replace all of the nutrients that plants need to thrive.

As for fisheries, recent studies have shown that over-fishing is decimating stocks of most fish that are important in the human diet. Ominous reports say that by the 2040s most will be gone. These are "renewable resources" that may become extinct if action is not taken soon. Hardship surely will fall on fishermen around the world in the next decades whether fishing is restricted to permit stocks to recover, or if over-fishing continues and various varieties become extinct.

HUMAN AND CULTURAL characteristics, as noted in Becker and Brubaker's questions 3 and 5, can also be understood as resources because they can advance or hold back human activities and improvements in a particular area. And, like natural resources, cultural resources (attitudes and beliefs that people hold, economic, educational, religious and other institutions humans have invented, and knowledge accumulated), vary widely from culture to culture, providing richness and experience to the tapestry of world cultures and history.

I am now a retired geography professor, and I might add that I am an "old-fashioned geographer". A few decades ago one of geography's research and teaching goals in a university curriculum was to help young students learn what the Earth was like in its diversity and potential and how humans use (and misuse) the Earth's resources. Geography departments in most universities and colleges offered world overview and "regional" courses focusing on major countries and continents. These courses were designed to help students learn about the world. However they have been set aside in recent decades as the discipline became computerized and fractionated. Only in the last few years with concerns about "terrorism" and climate change has there been a renewed interest in how people in their diverse cultures get along and how our lives are intertwined with all others around the planet.

For all high school and college students I believe a main purpose of studying geography still *should* be to help them understand at least those areas in the world that are in the news in all their beauty, diversity of environments, cultures and resources, as well as their problems. Geography should help people understand "how the world works" in terms of what actually is going on among nations, people and their institutions, the Earth's offerings, how well the people are being supported, and to identify ways by which people might have an opportunity for a better life.

With this point of view and despite Genesis I.28, the Earth must not be seen as something "given to people" to use as we wish. There are obvious limits to the Earth's offerings. The vast and growing gap between the "haves" and "have-nots" among the world's people and nations cannot be tolerated if we want "peace" and stability. These are matters of fairness and justice to our fellow "Earthlings".

President George W. Bush said "We fight against poverty because hope is an answer to terror". I would present that idea differently. I believe he should have said: "We should fight against poverty because eliminating poverty is THE MAIN answer to terror!" We must deal with poverty in ways that preserve the Earth's ability to "heal itself", so its bounty will be available not just for now but for all future generations. That last point speaks directly to the concern of this book: "How many people *can* the Earth support well in perpetuity?"

This Book. *Earth Is Overpopulated Now*" is organized in Parts A, B and C. This book's uniqueness is not so much in the information it presents, because much of it is widely known and already of concern to many people. Its uniqueness is in presenting it as a package from a geographer's point of view, with a focus on overpopulation, a message of urgency, and with the strong suggestion that *global law* through a Limited World Government—with Education and Religion as crucial aids—is the only practical avenue of solution for these global issues.

Part A deals with Earth resources that are of basic importance to the survival of individuals and the human family. Part A focuses on the "**People-Earth Equation**" and assesses the adequacy of each of the following in terms of supporting the human family into the future: Air, Water, Food and Fiber, Building Materials for shelter, and Energy. For each of these basics I share perspective information and discuss uses, problems, and some avenues of solution. I use the word "equation" to emphasize the complex relationships that *must be balanced* if humans are to establish a sustainable way of life on Earth.

Part B takes up the "**People-People Equation**" and focuses on three human institutions that have separated us from other animals, that "make us human", and have led to the flowering of culture. Institutions discussed include: Education, Religion (and the Arts), and Law. Each of these must make important contributions if the human family is to be successful in solving critical problems and developing the world's first true "civilization". Again I use the word "equation" to convey the need for humans to modify their education, beliefs and cultures so people will get along with each other—as they must—and adopt ways that will provide adequately for (a smaller) human family in perpetuity.

Part C begins with a chapter that summarizes Parts A and B in the consideration of the Earth-People Equation and the People-People Equation. The second chapter in Part C summarizes and adds points about the Overpopulation issue. A Concluding chapter and an Epilogue follow.

There are no footnotes in this book. Because of the complications of numbering and keeping track of footnotes as I write, I have included source information about quotes and other references as I use them. Additional reference information for each of the chapters is in "Bibliography and Selected References" in the back of the book.

*   *   *

By their very nature it should be very clear that the critical issues of our time are GLOBAL issues. None can be dealt with alone or by any nation alone. These issues include climate change and other Earth deteriorating indicators, dwindling reserves of petroleum, fresh water shortages, declining levels of living, population growth and overpopulation, unbridled corporate globalization, threatening pandemic diseases, and the increasingly costly and futile search for "security" through military might and wasteful war that by its nature can not solve problems.

So how should intelligent creatures respond to all of this? Should we continue in our usual routines and ignore these monumental life and civilization-threatening challenges that are pressing all around us? Or should we get our heads out of our everyday cocoons, push for action, and accept the risks and hard times that are sure to come as we take on these issues? There are going to be very hard and difficult times whether we do anything forward looking or not! We should take action NOW before the several crises arrive full force to direct the changes that will benefit all world citizens!

In his book, *The Long Emergency,* James H. Kunstler projects a grim future as it may unfold based on the depletion of fossil fuels. Al Gore's *An Inconvenient*

Truth focuses on global warming. In addition to these two critical issues, *Healing the World* discussed war and militarization and the greed of multinational corporations.

Left unattended, any one of these issues—including this book's emphasis on overpopulation—can bring civilization as we know it to its knees in only a decade or two. The fact that all of these issues are crying for a solution at the same time should not dishearten us. These issues should be taken up as a "cause for action" by everyone, but especially young people whose future is in jeopardy. I am convinced that a LIMITED GLOBAL GOVERNMENT is the only intelligent way for adults to resolve these *global crises*.

I do not take seriously the Bible's Armageddon or apocalyptic stories that come to us from times long ago when there was little ecological or world knowledge. Our future is up to us! If we ignore the realities about ourselves and our world today and our civilization collapses, it will not be because of a vengeful or disappointed God or because "Armageddon" has arrived. It will be because we humans have not used our intelligence and compassion to deal with the realities of our time. It will be because we ignore what we are doing to ourselves, to our neighbors on this planet, and to our Earth home itself.

There is no guarantee that we will be able to resolve all of these crises in time. However, if we have honest concern and compassion about the future of our children and grand children and those who will follow, we must try. The best we can do is at least begin to take action on the challenges that face the whole human family!

PART A: BASICS FOR SURVIVAL

Since humans became "human" with power to reflect and raise questions, we have largely taken our Earth home for granted—until the last several decades. The Earth is huge and offers much. It is our "home". In the past our forebears chose to live where basic needs could be provided close by. Though some day we may make settlements for a few on the moon and travel to other planets, the home base for the billions of humans will remain the Earth as long as the human species survives.

In Part A the physical basics and limitations of the Earth to support the human family are considered: air, water, land and other living things. Part A also includes a Chapter on Energy, especially fossil fuels that have spurred and supported the advances of the last three centuries. My conclusion in these considerations, and the conclusion of others, is that the Earth's bounty is limited in important ways and we must take action NOW if generations to come are to have a chance at a good life.

To set the stage for the issue of overpopulation, I begin with a brief perspective on how "life" may have come into being on Earth and elsewhere in the Universe and how living things evolved over billions of years to the diversity that enriches Planet Earth today.

Perspectives on the Beginning of Living Things. It is estimated that the Universe is about 15 billion years old and that the Earth was "born" about 4 or 5 billion years ago along with the other planets, forming out of our sun's nebula. Recent astronomical discoveries confirm the reality of many solar systems with planets in the universe and a steady evolutionary process of new stars, solar systems and even galaxies coming into being and dying.

When thinking about the Earth and its resources and how the human family is getting along, we must consider our probable uniqueness in the Universe. That uniqueness involves both the human family and the Earth itself. Given the probability that no other planet "out there" is exactly like our Earth, there is very little chance that life forms on other planets would have evolved to be like the variety we know on Earth. The unusual but human-like and human-sized characters in "Star Wars" are a virtual impossibility. And why should "life" only have evolved based on water and carbon as it has on Earth?

Why not intelligent creatures evolving on other planets, creatures that we would consider tiny—like ants, or gargantuan, depending in part on their planet's gravitation? Why not intelligent creatures with wings? Since life forms with more or less intelligence have evolved on Earth, it is just as likely that it has happened elsewhere in the universe under very different conditions and with very different manifestations of intelligence from what we think is "normal" on Earth.

Our planet is unique in its generally moderate temperatures. Living forms as we know them on Earth depend on liquid water. Since fairly early in its formation the Earth apparently had an abundance of water. We know that primitive life forms can survive next to very high temperature volcano spouts deep in the oceans. And many life forms are adapted to frigid Arctic and Antarctic conditions. However, research indicates that it was the temperature "window" between the conditions of freezing and boiling that made it possible for life *as we know it* to evolve on Earth and to proliferate to what we know today. Someone has said it was the "Goldilocks Factor"—not too hot and not too cold—that made life as we know it possible on Earth.

It is hypothesized that in the evolutionary process eons ago early life forms began in the water, and later some creatures moved onto the land. It has been established that the blood of mammals is about 1 % salt. It therefore can be further hypothesized that at the time when amphibious living forms shifted from water to land the salt level in their blood probably matched the ocean's salt content. Thus, the 1% salt level in our blood today might be a relic carried over from the time when early life forms living in water first developed circulation systems. Oceans are now about 3.4% salt by weight.

Research into the beginnings of all living things by Stanley Miller, Sidney Fox and others have demonstrated that complex proteins and primitive living cells can result from combining common amino acid components of protein with heat and water. Their research shows that by an internal self-organization process these primitive cells assemble themselves into cell-like structures of primitive proteins that can metabolize, grow, reproduce, and respond to stimuli.

These are characteristics of living things, not inert matter! And these primitive cell-like structures can perform all of these functions and activities without RNA or DNA. From such beginnings and over billions of years, these simplest of creations evolved to more and more complex living forms!

There are two reasons for mentioning research into the beginnings of life. One is simply to underscore how far evolution has taken the life process of Earth, leading from simple single cells—however they began—to the myriad forms of increasing complexity and abilities we see around us on Earth today, including ourselves.

The second and equally important reason is to emphasize that the evolution-ary process is ongoing. Conservation books used to note that "climax forms" of plant and animal communities evolved in different environments (ecological niches), with the implication that evolution had reached its climax and virtu-ally stopped. However, the evolutionary process continues on Earth and throughout the universe. Note how quickly some bacteria can evolve to survive the anti-bacterial drugs we invent and keep modifying to combat them! Assuming that our species survives, thousands of years from now humans will have evolved to be somewhat different from us in important ways and may have mental and other abilities we can only fantasize about now.

That point brings us back to the focus of this book. Our future depends entirely upon whether our worldwide human family is able to use its intelli-gence to develop a balance between the human family's demands on the Earth and how many humans the Earth can support at a reasonable level of living. Resolving this key issue depends on humans not wasting the Earth's treasure by warring among themselves, but learning to get along peacefully with each other and with all living things. This is a global issue. Somehow the people of the world must work together to achieve this balance, and soon, or else....

This Book's Part A considers the adequacy of essential resources provided by the Earth for the survival of all living things, but especially humans—regard-less of their wealth, power or poverty. Although arable land, fresh water and air are the most critical resource inputs for human survival, we must emphasize over and over that all aspects of the Earth's ecosystems are intricately interre-lated. Humans, therefore, must realize that every human action anywhere on Earth has repercussions on all natural systems.

Behind all of my comments is the question, "How many people can Earth's basic resources support?" Part A begins with Air because our need for oxygen is a constant and "minute by minute" need. The other needs, also very important, follow in the order of their urgency for our survival as individuals and as a species.

CHAPTER 1

ATMOSPHERE—OXYGEN

Of all of Earth's resources oxygen (O2) is the one needed constantly by humans and other creatures. Every few moments, every day of our lives we must inhale oxygen to survive. Air is so essential to life that each person should have a "natural right" to fresh air. Wherever we are the condition of the atmosphere around us is of utmost importance.

Our Earth's atmosphere, our "air", is now about 21% oxygen, but it has not always been that way. The gas mixture that enveloped the early Earth was made up mostly of methane, ammonia and water vapor. After several billion years, various forms of algae were the first plant life able to use chlorophyll to convert sunlight into energy and oxygen. With increasing plant life oxygen slowly became a significant portion of the Earth's atmosphere.

About a half billion years ago the oxygen in the atmosphere set the stage for evolution of other creatures, an evolutionary process that has continued. During the last half billion years the portion of oxygen in the atmosphere varied from lows near 10% and a high of about 35%. When the oxygen level was high, as during the Carboniferous Age, plants and some creatures (dinosaurs) proliferated and grew to gargantuan size. When oxygen level was low there were mass extinctions and only smaller sized living things were able to survive.

The 21% oxygen we now have therefore is a middling number. In addition to the oxygen, our atmosphere is 78% nitrogen, an inert but very important gas, so oxygen and nitrogen total about 99% of our "air". The last 1% is mostly inert argon gas, with other gases in very small amounts.

Atmospheric temperatures also have varied considerably through time. About 12,000 years ago (and over just a few years) world temperatures dropped between 20 and 30 degrees, and remained down for centuries. We now are in a period of rapid temperature increase, which, unless it is reversed, will impact all life on Earth in the decades and centuries ahead.

We should never forget the symbiotic relationship between Earth's plants and animals. About 70% of our oxygen comes from algae and other chemical actions taking place in the oceans. The rest of our oxygen comes from forests and other land plants that take in and use carbon dioxide and give off oxygen. In contrast to plants using carbon dioxide and giving off oxygen, animals in their living processes need and use oxygen and give off carbon dioxide, a neat symbiotic arrangement. The millions of fossil fuel-using vehicles and machines humans have invented have increased the amount of carbon dioxide in the atmosphere. In using oxygen and giving off carbon dioxide, automobiles and other vehicles therefore are like millions more large animals who are living off the Earth's fossil fuels ("ancient sunshine"). The carbon dioxide increase in the atmosphere is the primary cause of the Earth's rapid climate change and "global warming".

For the survival of the human family and other creatures on which we depend (like bees, butterflies, domestic animals) we must pay close attention to the health and welfare of the entire plant kingdom and the oceans on which we also depend. There must be a balance among all forms of life. The great organist, philosopher and medical missionary in Africa, Albert Schweitzer, taught us we must have "Reverence for Life", and he meant all life!

Air Pollution. Because air is so essential and yet so widely available in the natural environment, we don't think about it often—unless there is a local problem. Until only a few decades ago it was thought that "air" was an unlimited resource, and in a way it still is. However, mostly as the result of human actions, the air has become polluted, especially in and around large cities.

A mantle of air about ten miles deep covers the whole Earth and until recent decades it was assumed that, in its abundance and movement, air would clean itself of human-made pollution. Los Angeles, Pittsburgh and Donora, Pennsylvania, Copperhill, Tennessee, and Bangkok, Thailand, come to mind as cities that have been in the news over the years because of air pollution and deaths attributed to air pollution.

Especially in and around the world's larger cities the quality of our air resource has been polluted and our efforts to correct that have been feeble. Many people do not know that because of the concentration of people, machines, furnaces and air conditioners, areas in and around the world's cities also have become "heat islands", with average temperatures several degrees higher than surrounding areas.

In 1970 the United States passed a "Clean Air Act" and significant progress was made in the following decades to reduce air pollution. In 1990 during the first George Bush's presidency, the Clean Air Act was modified and improved, and in 1997 President Clinton tightened some of the Act's standards still further. In 2002 President George W. Bush proposed a "Clear Skies Initiative" which, contradictory to its name, would have significantly reversed much of the pollution reduction progress that was made in recent decades. President George W. Bush's misnamed "Clear Skies Initiative" was not enacted by Congress, but the President went ahead with reduced standards by Executive Order. Studies show that the quality of air over the United States has deteriorated since 2001.

Discovery of the Ozone Hole over Antarctica was a wake-up call to the world. Since the invention of refrigerators and air conditioners chlorofluorocarbon (CFC) gases were commonly used as the refrigerant. When very lightweight CFC gases are released they rise to the stratosphere and destroy the ozone layer that shields all living things from harmful ultra violet radiation. Gases from fossil fuel burning, mostly carbon dioxide, also rise to deplete the Ozone shield in the upper atmosphere.

Responding to this serious problem, 180 nations agreed to the Montreal Protocol of 1987 that set targets to eliminate use of CFCs and use instead alternative gases that have been developed. The international agreement called for phasing out the damaging gases by 2005. It was projected that the ozone hole would then be "repaired" by the year 2040 or 2050.

With less than 5% of the world's population, the United States, with its heavy dependence on oil, coal and gas for transportation and industry, is responsible for over 25% of the world's total air pollution, the highest of any nation. A conference was held in Kyoto, Japan, in the late 1990s for nations to reach agreement for phased cuts of 5.2% in "greenhouse gas" emissions, mostly carbon dioxide, by the year 2012. Many nations signed the Kyoto Protocol, including President Clinton for the United States. In one of his early acts as President, George W. Bush withdrew the U.S. support from the Kyoto

Protocol. The Kyoto agreement waited seven years, until 2005, for enough (other) nations to ratify it so it could enter into force. By 2005 141 nations that account for 55% of worldwide greenhouse gas emissions had ratified the agreement.

As of June 2006 the United States and Australia are the only industrialized nations that have not ratified the Kyoto Protocol. However, recent studies indicate that because of increases in fossil fuel use in several countries, carbon dioxide emissions are on the rise and may reach a "tipping point" after which it will be very difficult to eliminate them. All living things on Earth therefore could be subject to increased eye damage and skin cancer.

Earth Climate Change/ Global Warming. The atmosphere, our weather and our climate are obviously involved with the Earth's climate change and "Global Warming". "Greenhouse Gases" also are frequently in the news about global warming.

We should not think about greenhouse gases only in a negative way. Life on Earth depends on greenhouse gases. Just like the glass covering a greenhouse, a stratospheric layer of mixed gases for billions of years has kept the Earth's temperature warmer than it otherwise would be. Our atmosphere holds heat in and keeps Earth temperatures within a relatively narrow range. All living things depend on the stability of that narrow range of temperature to survive (the Earth's "Goldilocks Factor" that was mentioned). The mix of natural "greenhouse" gases that helps keep us warm and shields us from solar radiation include: Water vapor, carbon dioxide, methane, ozone (in very small quantities) and nitrous oxide.

The global warming problem of our time results from changes in the mix of gases that form this atmospheric shield. The Industrial Revolution brought on massive use of fossil fuels that has increased carbon dioxide and nitrous oxide in the atmosphere. As was noted, the use of CFCs in industry and refrigeration reduced the ozone content in the atmosphere, caused the "ozone hole", and the world's response was the Montreal Protocol.

For years research has confirmed the rise in average global temperatures that is slowly modifying our planet's climate. An article in *Science News* (Feb. 9, 1991) cites borehole research in 1986 by geophysicist Arthur Lachenbruch that demonstrated a 2 to 4 degree (Centigrade) increase during the twentieth century. There have been many swings between warmer and colder eras in Earth history. However, it is a new phenomenon that intensive human use of fossil fuels has released smoke and exhaust fumes in amounts that can no longer be "cleaned" by the Earth's natural processes. Studies of ancient ice cores confirm that the carbon dioxide content of the atmosphere has risen in recent decades to levels the Earth has not seen for 50,000 years.

We would be recklessly foolish to ignore such a basic phenomenon that even now may be beyond any human ability to reverse it. Assuming it continues, it will disrupt so much of what humans do and where and how we do it around the world. Large areas of most of the world's major cities have been built close to sea level. With a rise in sea level of only a few feet these low lying areas will be swamped, overwhelming the homes of millions of people and completely disrupting the function of world ports and ocean shipping, so vital to civilization as we know it. Large areas of the world's most productive farmlands also are at relatively low elevations and vulnerable to a rising sea level. Global warming will change the length of the growing season, storm patterns and drought and flooding probabilities in many parts of the world. The purpose of Al Gore's movie and book, *An Inconvenient Truth*, is to inform us about these critical possibilities.

A rise in the average level of the Earth's oceans of several feet would shrink Florida's peninsula by about a third, eliminating tourist havens and many of Florida's special agricultural areas. Global warming may change the movement of the Gulf Stream, possibly cutting off its warming of western and northern Europe and the United Kingdom. The result of such a shift would leave Europe and the United Kingdom with a climate similar to much of Canada, with devastating long-term effects. Although climate changes so far have been gradual, changes in the world's oceans could pass a "tipping point" at any time and bring on major changes world wide in only a few years.

Solutions? First about air pollution, what can and must be done to restore our atmosphere's purity and make sure it remains "clean", or at least clean enough, for all time?

Somewhere I read that, just as mammals have two lungs, the Earth also has two "lung" systems: the forests and oceans. Forests and oceans "manufacture" oxygen and oceans eliminate pollution and clean the air. If humans are to survive as a species we must protect the forests and oceans for our own long-term survival. I will have more to say about that in chapters about "water" and "food-fiber".

We can no longer fall back on the notion that air is an unlimited resource that will "clean itself". Legislative efforts seeking improvements and controls like our 1970 Clean Air Act and international agreements such as the Montreal Protocol and the Kyoto Protocol must be taken seriously and strengthened, despite negative effects on some activities and the "bottom line" of some industries. Note and keep in mind Appendix E3, a list of "Ethical Points for the Future", one of which says, "Harmony with nature is more important than economic progress."

Harmony with nature is critically important because the future of the human family and how well our children and grandchildren will be able to live are at stake. Again the United States' non-participation in and non-compliance with the Kyoto Protocol come to mind. We should not ignore reasonable and necessary local, national or global environmental standards or goals for the sake of immediate inconvenience, profits, or even jobs. It is encouraging that dozens of U.S. cities have taken action on their own to comply with the Kyoto Protocol standards. A sustainable future for everyone is worth sacrifices today.

Virtually all air conditioners now use gases that do not contribute to the destruction of the ozone layer in the stratosphere. Hopefully, the hole in the ozone, that had developed in recent decades from the use of R-12 refrigerant, may be repaired in the years ahead, thus restoring the shield that protects all living things on Earth from radiation that causes damage to eyes and skin.

Corporations will complain that if environmental standards are raised they will not be able to compete in the world's markets. That is a short-term excuse. Even higher air pollution standards must be set by a revised Kyoto Protocol or by the U.N. and monitored. If all polluting industries—world-wide—follow new standards, none will be advantaged over another. They all will be operating on a more level playing field. If we fail to take care of our air, fresh water and arable land, the human experiment on Earth may soon be on its knees.

Adjusting to new ways and more stringent air pollution standards will be a challenge. The best we can do is help industries that have problems in adjusting to new standards to make necessary changes over a very few years as they find ways to remain economically viable. There will be hard times for some industries and for workers who must find new employment. But on the other hand, there will be new jobs that must be filled as we become more concerned about the long-term health of our planet as well as the health and well being of the human family.

As for global warming, a quote by Camille Parmesan in the Sept-Oct. 2005 *Audubon* explains why the only way we have a chance at reversing it is by global action:

> "Climate change is fundamentally different (from other problems pressing on the human family) because it is the only one (natural system) you cannot locally do anything about. There is no restoration technique or local management option that allows you to reverse it … It (dealing with climate change) will take a huge collective effort, globally, and that makes it very scary for conservation."

We humans don't have the time or money to continue exhaustive and expensive wars that waste everything, solve nothing and cause more conflict. The world's PEOPLE must come together as reasonable adults to deal with ominous climate changing prospects. Could restrictions on gas guzzling vehicles and support of public transport reduce global warming? Yes! Can careful regulation of smoke emissions and other measures retard or stop the Earth's slow temperature increase? Would more walking and use of bicycles help? All of these would help.

Can we really protect urban shorelines and low lying areas—like New Orleans—with higher and still higher and more expensive levees? No. Can critical structures be rebuilt on higher ground? Probably some. And all of this must be done at whose expense? These are "global warming" questions that rational leaders and all people must take seriously and soon.

Parmesan's note that it will take *global action* to deal with air pollution, global warming and other Earth based problems underscores the need for a Limited Global Government that has been empowered to deal with these global issues.

This chapter's obvious conclusion is that there is no shortage of "air" on Earth. The problems are the air pollution especially over major cities, that human actions are changing the chemical composition of air, and that these changes can seriously affect the health and survival of all living things, including humans.

CHAPTER 2

FRESH WATER

A large portion of every mammal is "water". Part of that water is incorporated in the closed system of our blood stream that is recycled and, except for blood loss from accidents, needs little replenishment. However, our bodies have two systems that demand several quarts or liters of fresh water each day. One of these is our digestive and personal waste disposal system. The other is our temperature control system that keeps our bodies at a constant optimum temperature by perspiration. The human body can survive weeks without food; only days without water.

Water covers about three-fourths of the Earth's surface and one might think that water, like air, is an "unlimited" natural resource. However, ninety-seven and a half percent of the world's water is in the salt-laden oceans. Only about two and a half percent of the Earth's water is "fresh", and most of that (until recent global warming) is locked up in glaciers, mountain top snow packs, and in the two polar regions in ice, snow and permafrost. That leaves only about half of one percent of the world's water that is available to be used over and over through the hydrologic cycle by every living thing on the Earth.

In contrast to some other resources, we do not "consume" fresh water in the same way we consume food or use up energy from fossil fuels. After it has been used, virtually all fresh water goes "back around" in the Earth's continuous natural hydrologic cycle that involves our atmosphere, snow and rainfall, storms, evaporation, rivers, lakes, oceans, glaciers, and ice-caps. Some of it also seeps into the ground and moves slowly as "ground water". Like "air", fresh water can—and must—be used again and again. The fresh water we use today has been used and reused since the beginnings of life of Earth by all plants and animals in all their functions.

In this introduction about water, the importance of mountains and winter snows must be emphasized. Obviously mountain areas are important for forestry, mining, recreation and other uses; however they may be even more important as water storage and release areas. Areas at lower elevations are dependant on the gradual spring and summer release of water from winter snows at higher elevations. That is especially true of areas with climates that are called "Mediterranean" (Southern California, areas around the Mediterranean Sea, etc.). These areas receive virtually all of their precipitation in the winter months and must depend entirely on gradual release of melting snows from nearby upland areas during spring and summer growing seasons.

Fresh water is super abundant in some places on the Earth, is a very limited resource in other places, and is virtually unavailable in many other places. In recent decades there has been growing tension between water surplus areas and other places that have very little or no water. A long article by Michael Specter in the October 23, 2006, *New Yorker* (page 67 plus) informs us that the Chinese character for "political order" is based on the symbol for water, with the obvious connection that those who control the water, control the people.

Water Uses and Needs in the Past. The availability and transportability of water would have been as important as food wherever early humans settled or traveled. From their beginnings all human settlements—for survival—located close to a dependable fresh water source, such as a spring, river or lake. All mobility was by walking (or being carried!) on land or being moved on water by simple boats or rafts.

In order to travel away from well-watered settlements or to move about and settle in drier areas, early people became very creative in inventing ways to catch, store, carry and move fresh water in skin bags, large jars, cisterns, tanks, elaborate networks of ditches, canals, and qanats and foggaras (man-made underground tunnels and channels). Devices, like the Archimedes screw and the shadouf, also were (and are) used to facilitate irrigation in the drier parts of the world.

Per capita water consumption around the world increased very slowly over the millennia. In the early days of the human saga on Earth, it is likely that humans used only enough water to quench their thirst and for occasional washing, much as animals we see around us do now.

It is estimated that when the Agricultural Revolution began in about 8000 BCE there were 5,000,000 humans scattered in small groups around the world and their demands on local water supplies would have been minimal. Surface streams, rivers, lakes and shallow wells provided fresh water for planted fields and for use in and around human habitations, and (later) craft shops in villages and towns.

In towns and cities folks came to public wells until on-site pumps and city water systems became commonplace. In farming areas family members trudged each day to fill their pails and jugs at a river, spring or well nearby until late in the 1800s when the ubiquitous "windmill" was invented. Until the last two centuries a daily use of about 10 gallons per person was adequate.

Major cities in centuries past built impressive systems that drew water from higher ground miles away. Elaborate aqueduct systems were used in ancient times to supply water to some cities around the Mediterranean Sea and the Near East (A better name for the Middle East). Remnants of some of these are visible today. Early cities like Rome had public baths, latrines and fountains, and studies have shown that the overall supply in ancient Rome provided about 17 gallons of water per day per person. It also is technologically impressive—even with the health problems they no doubt unknowingly caused—that in the centuries BCE cities like Rome and Pompeii had lead pipe systems for delivering water to the villas of wealthier families.

Recent Increases in Water Uses. The Industrial Revolution changed everything, including not only the way of life in Europe, the United States and a few other countries, but it also brought on a sharp increase in the use of water. Instead of crafts being carried on in homes or small shops, large factories were first located beside rivers or canals where water power, by intricate systems of belts and wheels, could be applied to run many machines in the same building.

The invention of the steam engine in 1775 made it possible to locate factories away from water and brought on the spread of towns and factories. A network of man-made canals first, and then railroads, were used to move people, to supply the factories with needed resources and to move products of the factories to markets. Large factories and railroads were the driving forces of the Industrial Revolution in England, Western Europe and the United States. Late in the nineteenth century more efficient gasoline-driven internal combustion engines were adopted to generate power and they dominate transportation on rails and roads around the world to this day.

The mechanization of agriculture—in effect a Second Agricultural Revolution—increased farm production and brought on increases in population and the demand for more fresh water. With the increase in use of fresh water around the world, the streams, rivers and lakes that provided ample water in the past now have become used to their limits, some even beyond their limits. Wells supplemented water supplies for cities and farmers, and some farmers, needing more water than rainfall and the common windmills could pump from shallow wells, dug deep wells to supplement natural precipitation on their fields.

In addition to an increase in food production, the Industrial Revolution was accompanied by the application of science to the medical profession, stimulating a virtual Medical Revolution. Increased water use and purification had other dynamic repercussions on the lives of those in industrializing towns and cities and mechanizing farms. In earlier times, birth rates and death rates both were high. However, with sterilization and more water for cleaning and sanitation, death rates dropped and populations grew rapidly.

As they have grown, cities in humid areas purchased large tracts of land in uplands nearby and built dams so they could impound and control the runoff from a stream's watershed. In dry areas, as in Western U.S., large dams and reservoirs were constructed by governments, and some farmers and ranchers in dry areas have found it profitable in recent years to sell their land with water rights to expanding cities and towns. But even with these strategies, shortages have continued as still more fresh water is always needed.

Manufacturing and household uses do not account for most of the fresh water used in the United States. Irrigation farming in our western states uses over 75% of our fresh water, which comes from reservoirs on major rivers and from groundwater sources. Although for centuries irrigation has been used in dry areas to raise high value crops, much of the irrigated land in the U.S.'s West and Midwest is used to raise grains and other crops that have a relatively low return per acre. This is possible because the cost of water for irrigation to farmers and ranchers in our western states is subsidized by the government from government-built reservoirs. U.S. farmers using "supplementary irrigation" also are advantaged by special tax rates that apply to depletion of groundwater supplies.

Regardless of whether impounded surface water or groundwater is used, in dry areas the salinization of soils has always been a problem with irrigation farming. The flushing action of natural precipitation eliminates this problem in humid areas, but it is a constant problem in dry areas. Salinization of soils has been cited as an important cause of the decline of the early Sumerian, Babylonian and Assyrian civilizations in the Near East that depended heavily on irrigation. In recent decades salinization has caused abandonment of some irrigation farming lands in western U.S. and elsewhere in the world.

Surface and groundwater sources, besides being used more heavily, have been further compromised by the runoff of pesticides, herbicides and fertilizers from farmlands. Large scale corporate agribusiness operations appear to be efficient because negative effects on ecological systems are not figured into their balance sheets. (Environmental problems caused by these farms are considered in the next chapter.) In cities, runoff of chemicals from factories and food processing plants and sewage dumping present ongoing water problems, along with salt and ice-melting materials in northern areas.

Fresh water demand no longer is limited to what each person needs each day for drinking, bathing, cleaning and sanitation. Actual direct "people use" of water in the U.S. is over 100 gallons per day, far more than the generally agreed upon minimum personal need of 12 gallons per day. Numerous water using appliances and cleanliness habits now have become almost a necessity in "western countries". These include the habit of many people in the United States of taking a daily shower or bath and our frequent use of flush toilets. Included also are our ubiquitous fountains and our common use of water-using dishwashers, automatic clothes washing machines and garbage disposers in homes. Even as these appliances have been improved to use less water (and energy), the total they add to our use of fresh water is great.

Many industrial processes themselves use large amounts of water. For example, it is estimated that it takes about 1,500 gallons of water to produce the beef, bun and other items in a hamburger with fries and soft drink. Other estimates indicate it takes 1,800 gallons of water to raise the cotton and produce a pair of jeans, 32,000 gallons of water to produce the steel that goes into an average automobile, and about 50 gallons of water to produce 1 gallon of gasoline. It is no small wonder that industrialized nations have increased their use of water many times in recent decades, and it is no surprise that supplying sufficient fresh water, especially to major cities, has become such a challenge. Average daily per capita use of fresh water in the United States, which includes residential, industrial and irrigation uses, has been over 1500 gallons in recent years.

One fifth of the land that was planted in the Great Plains of the United States in the 1970s is no longer "farmed" for lack of water, and another fifth is expected to no longer be available for planted crops by 2020, again for lack of water. When the cost of pumping underground water to the surface exceeds the value of crops that might be raised by the pumped water, land is shifted from cropping by supplementary irrigation back to range and pasture. From Texas to Montana underground water supplies from the Ogallala Aquifer have been used many times faster than their slow replenishment from the Rocky Mountains. In a few decades these areas will again become rangeland for ranchers, as they were during the 1800s, and they will support far fewer people. Surplus population living on farms and in towns and cities in these areas will pose a challenging problem for local, state and national governments.

Since World War II the world's population has become far more urbanized and water demanding in both "developed" and "developing" countries. In 2000, many dozens of cities were over a million in population, several dozen were over ten million, and the largest, Tokyo, Mexico City and New York with their suburbs, had populations of about thirty million each! It always has been a challenge to provide a dependable supply of fresh water for cities, but the challenge is virtually impossible with massive and growing concentrations of people and industries, as well as for handling the daily generation of human and industrial waste materials. Several of the world's largest cities already employ very restrictive rationing. Strange as it may seem, these gargantuan cities still attract thousands and thousands more people each year.

In his book, *Tapped Out*, Senator Paul Simon cites a World Bank study which informs us that 22 nations had "severe" water problems in the 1990s and 80 more had "serious" problems. Paul Simon also notes that by 2020 thirty-five nations will have severe water shortages. Several Near Eastern countries already depend on desalinization for all or part of their water needs. In all Near East countries water supply is the common problem, stemming largely from steady population increases. In the United States and Europe, industrial expansion and pollution are the more important water issues. Senator Simon also wrote that the next wars are likely to be "water wars". And that is likely if humans do not abandon war as a failed strategy for solving international disputes. Again the need for a Limited Global Government!

Large and small lakes are drying up all over the world. Global warming doubt-less is one cause. But more and still more water from streams and rivers is being used by cities and farms, so less water is available to maintain lake levels. Already in the Earth's most populous and driest areas so much water is drawn from some rivers that very little or none ever reaches an ocean or sea. The Colorado River in southwest U.S. is one example. The United States and Mexico have long standing agreements that a certain volume of "fresh" water will flow to Mexico from the Colorado River. However, there have been prob-lems of salinity and many years when Mexico receives no water. China's mas-sive Yellow River rarely delivers water to the Yellow Sea.

Other Problems Related to Water. In the preceding pages we have noted some of the primary problems relating to our looming water crisis. There are still more issues that make solving these problems difficult. Groundwater sources near oceans and seas have the additional problem of "salt water intrusion". If the amount of fresh water drawn from the ground exceeds natural fresh water recharging rates, salt water will seep in from the ocean to take the place of the fresh water that has been pumped out, thereby salinizing and ruining the groundwater source.

An additional problem with ground water sources is that the aquifers (the porous rocks deep underground that are saturated with water) may be weak-ened when water is pumped out. If enough water is pumped out and recharg-ing is slow, the weight of the overburden of other Earth materials above can cause the aquifer rocks to collapse. The U.S. Geological Survey reports that land subsidence from ground water withdrawal has happened in virtually every state. When aquifers collapse they are closed forever from recharging and are no longer "renewable natural resources".

Salinization of irrigated lands was mentioned as a problem, and the solution to salinization is a "Catch-22" situation. Flushing accumulated salts is possible, but it requires large quantities of fresh water. But that is the Catch-22 problem. The reason these areas are using irrigation in the first place is because they are water short areas.

Still another problem is disposal of urban waste materials. In the past some cities dumped waste materials in the ocean, a practice banned since the early 1980s. However some cities now are pumping liquefied waste materials into the ground, deep enough in the ground so that, hopefully, they will cause no future problem. These practices are not wise, given how much we do not know about the Earth's crust and crustal movements and the problems we already face from groundwater pollution.

In the previous chapter I mentioned the significant increase in the atmosphere's carbon dioxide component. Absorption of carbon dioxide by the oceans creates carbonic acid and thereby slowly but steadily increases the acidity of the oceans. The increasing acidity is eliminating coral reefs and compromising the health of plankton and small shellfish which, in turn, impacts the food supply of marine creatures higher on the food chain. (Internet item http://www.washingtonpost.com/wp-dyn/content/article/2006/07/04/AR2006070400772_pf)

Regarding fresh water, the portent for the future is not good. Over half of China's food is raised by irrigation, about thirty per cent of India's, and all of Egypt's, and their populations and industries are growing along with their need for fresh water! In India large government sponsored reservoir construction projects funded by the World Bank have displaced thousands of villagers. In her book, *Power Politics*, Arundhati Roy relates the tragedy of dam development in India. She writes that, despite promises, villagers displaced by construction of a dam get little help from their government in resettling or finding employment, and after dam projects are completed the villagers must purchase water they need to survive.

As a final note on the world's mounting problems involving fresh and ocean water, climate change is happening. Although the Earth's hydrologic cycle will continue to function, climate change and global warming will add water from melting of the ice caps and glaciers to the oceans. Further, it is predicted that climate change will alter the normal precipitation and seasonal patterns of temperature of many places, making some areas drier or wetter, cooler or warmer. The increased evaporation from warmer temperatures will raise the atmosphere's vapor load and trigger more severe storms in some areas, drought in others.

Global warming also will increase the demand for energy and thereby the use of air conditioning in some areas, especially cities, and the "heat island" effect will further increase warming in localized urban areas. In contrast to the average increase in Earth temperatures, a shift in the Gulf Stream may cause a significant cooling of Europe, completely disrupting the way of life of hundreds of millions of people in the new European Union, Russia, Ukraine and other countries to the east.

Solving the Fresh Water Shortage Problem? Is there a single solution to this critical global fresh water problem? Or are there multiple solutions that together might provide the solution? It has to be the latter. As Paul Simon said in *Tapped Out*, there is no simple or single solution for our water needs or problems. We must combine a host of smaller efforts—with legal "teeth"— toward more efficient use, reuse, and conservation. To make all of these efforts helpful for our children and the long term we also must take action as a global community to stabilize and reduce the Earth's population.

How many people can the world's fresh water resources support on a sustainable basis? The prospect of the world's population increasing to 8 or 9 billion by 2050 presents an impossible challenge to provide an ever-increasing supply of fresh water for all of its many uses.

There are too many variables to come up with a firm answer. However, we know for sure: Large and small cities as well as some regions and nations with many millions of people already are having great difficulty in providing their inhabitants with a dependable supply of fresh water at reasonable cost. In some countries water is available for only certain hours during the week. One of the U.N.'s eight Millennium Development Goals is to reduce by half by 2015 the number of people *who do not* have access to clean water, but little progress has been made toward that goal up to 2006.

There is much we humans can do to alleviate our fresh water problems. The economic engine of an unbridled market economy, with its premise of constant growth and promise of more gadgets, with many industrial processes requiring huge amounts of fresh water, with many water-using "labor saving devices" in our homes, must be reigned in. Stemming the drive for constant growth in everything, *including population*, must be a key part of any long-term solution to resolving our fresh water and other problems related to natural resources.

Profit-seeking international corporations are purchasing water rights and city water systems. In her book, *Water Wars*, Indian activist Vandana Shiva instructs us that resources, like water that is needed for survival, should not be privatized but should be developed as the common wealth (and need) of the people. As was mentioned at the beginning of the chapter on AIR, many believe having adequate fresh air is a natural right of being a citizen of the Earth, and water also should be a basic right of citizenship. It is encouraging that in some places, like Bolivia, the people and their government have prevailed and cancelled contracts with water supplying corporations that had begun to gouge the public with higher and higher water rates.

There are very serious local, national and regional problems needing attention that involve distribution of water and national boundaries, especially to our larger cities. We are crowding too many people in large cities for any reasonable plan to provide a dependable long-term supply of fresh water to every person at a reasonable price. The question must be raised about our "throwaway consumerism". Do we need all of those products and, if so, can processes be developed that use less water? The elimination of leakage in city systems should be a continuing high priority in city management. Again referring to *Tapped Out*, Paul Simon cites Amman, Jordan's capitol city, where 59% of the water was lost in the system, probably by leakage or pilferage, and "unaccounted for". Other cities also have significant losses.

Ground water or surface water used for irrigation should be used only to raise high value crops, and farmers using irrigation should pay a fair price for their water. And we must get used to repurifying and reusing our fresh water over and over!

Other avenues of solution to imminent water shortage problems involve increasing the efficiency of water used for personal needs, limiting ground water use, and control by the people through their governments of ownership of water rights and systems. Each of these will have serious economic implications for those whose livelihoods will be affected. And that, again, is why the issue of overpopulation should compel our attention!

Desalinization of ocean water is becoming more competitive as the cost of providing fresh water from the usual surface and ground water sources rises. A few ocean-fronting areas like Kuwait, Israel and California already are augmenting their fresh water supplies by desalinization. Development of a less costly and solar powered desalinization system would be as important for the human family as learning to use fire was eons ago. Developing such a desalinization technology would be far more important for a peaceful future for mankind than designing or building a more lethal fighter airplane. More scientists should be encouraged by governments to take up this quest.

However, there is a potential downside. In pursuing the quest for more efficient desalinization, we must realize that, vast as are the oceans, ultimately they too are limited. They provide most of the carbon dioxide to oxygen conversion and are an important food source. However, over time and if the use of desalinization increases significantly, the salt content of the oceans is likely to rise in particular areas, destroying local ocean ecosystems.

The "bottom line" of this chapter is: The Earth's fresh water resources are limited and very unevenly distributed. There are many water related and other issues that need resolution and Global Warming will only add to the looming crises! Inasmuch as many water problems are international, development of a Limited Global Government would provide the best framework for resolution of those issues, and for the long-term survival of the human family.

CHAPTER 3

FOOD AND FIBER

With air being "everywhere", the availability of food and fresh water was the key factor in determining locations where humans originally settled the Earth. In more recent times, human concerns relating to food and water have also involved land fertility, farm, fish and forestry techniques and availability of fertilizers. Other critical "availability of food" factors (not addressed in this book) involve tenure and ownership of farmland, government programs, transportation facilities, foreign trade and more.

Before taking up the world's capacity to produce food, fiber and fish—and relating these to human needs—we constantly must remind ourselves that all of the Earth's environments function as a whole.

I keep reminding us that we humans must pay attention to all of the Earth's lands and oceans because what happens everywhere on Earth has an effect on "how the natural world works" in terms of the progression of the seasons, on precipitation amounts and in what form it comes, on erosion, on global warming, and doubtless other factors. We must pay attention to the impact of our actions on all mountains, the tropical rain forests, Arctic and Antarctic areas including the thinly settled boreal forests in northern Canada and Russia, as well as lakes, rivers, seas and the oceans.

We must pay attention to all of these as we use the Earth's resources because all elements of the natural environment are intricately interrelated everywhere on Earth in ways we do not fully understand. The onset of the apparent rapid climate change in recent decades is a case in point. In large part it is the result of our unwitting use over a century and a half of fossil fuels in our homes, factories and millions of vehicles, an "addiction" for which we must find alternatives very soon! The sustainable balance that must be established between People and the Earth (the "People-Earth Equation") therefore must include the whole Earth, including areas so far relatively unaffected by human activities.

The title of this chapter mentions food and fiber, but most attention is given to food production. Production of fibers, like cotton, flax, and wool, are part of the total farming enterprise but do not figure as importantly as the availability of food in the settlement patterns of humans on Earth. Man-made filaments, like nylon, also are not discussed. These new "fibers", many made from petroleum products, are not part of the farming enterprise. Their production in the future will depend on the availability and price of petroleum.

With the energy crisis in recent years "product competition" for farmland also has become an important factor in agricultural production and decision-making. Grain and other farm products may have several possible uses: as food for humans, food for animals, as industrial raw materials, as "biofuels" for our vehicles, for making liquors, or for export. The energy crisis also now impinges directly on farming in an additional way because "farmers" no longer grow fuel for their own "horsepower". They are as dependent as city dwellers on purchasing all of their energy needs!

Food and the Proliferation of Life. During the billions of years when simple life forms were proliferating and increasing in numbers and complexity and were spreading around the Earth, the numbers of any species were kept in balance by various natural limiting factors, especially the food supply. To accommodate for the high natural attrition rate in all living things, "Nature" has always provided far more seeds and young plants and animals than are expected to grow up and become reproductive themselves. Numbers of all plants and creatures were and are kept in check by limitations on food supply and water, by predations of other creatures that use other living things for their food supply, by plague, and by negative mutational "glitches" in DNA as it has been "handed down". Large and small natural disasters also would have taken toll of many living things. Until the last few centuries these same limiting factors applied to humans.

In all species, including humans, Darwin"s "natural selection" process would have led to a constant thinning of the weaker, the deformed, and those with negative mutational changes, thus leaving propagation of later generations to the more robust and able survivors and those with positive mutational changes that gave them a survival advantage.

For perhaps millions of years hunting, gathering, fishing and perhaps roaming with a few domesticated animals were the "way of life" of a few hundred thousand "pre-humans" in scattered places around the Earth. Innovation, change and the spread of pre-humans around the world happened slowly, and through the lives of most people the changes were few, usually small and not disruptive. It is likely that innovative individuals who pushed too hard for making a change were not treated well. (Are things much different now—with innovators and whistleblowers?) Life was precarious and birth and death rates must have been about equal. People made shelters and tools from natural materials available locally. Contact with other groups for trade was important but minimal.

As was noted, "farming" was invented about 8000 years ago in several places including the Near East, and the world's human population at that time is estimated to have been about 5 million. Like learning to use fire, the planting of seeds where humans chose to plant them and tending those plants to fruition was a major milestone in fending off starvation and the development of settled populations in villages. Even after the beginning of the "Agricultural Revolution" humans and their small communities functioned largely as part of the natural environment. The survival rate of humans increased with a more dependable food supply. Work was done by animal or human muscles or by water wheels or wind. Human and animal waste was used for fertilizer.

The invention of farming increased the food supply and led to a steady but slow increase in the human population, which by 1 CE had reached a total of about 170 million. Further improvements in agricultural techniques were spread around the world, and two thousand years later humans farm virtually all of the Earth's arable (tillable, crop raising) land and have settled most other environments, some very thinly.

As population continued to grow, larger villages and towns were established in places with particular advantages. Some people became specialists and the level of innovation and creativity increased. With further increases in population—and not comprehending the consequences—human actions caused the spread the deserts in North Africa, the Near East, India and China. Humans virtually eliminated the "cedars of Lebanon" and the forests of Greece and the rest of Europe. The same is happening even now with human clearing of tropical rain forests.

The Industrial Revolution, which began in England in the late 1700s, brought on important and remarkable inventions in industry and agriculture, especially in the United States and Europe. The Industrial Revolution triggered an enormous increase in world population. Whereas the earlier Agricultural Revolution had triggered an increase in the survival rate of humans, the Industrial Revolution triggered the Medical Revolution that brought on a reduction in the death rate and a rapid increase in population.

In 1798 the population of the world had reached about 900 million and, viewing with dismay the living conditions and population increase in England, Thomas Malthus wrote the "Essay on Population". The essay points out that, even considering the many ways in which the number of humans may be held in check by wars, starvation and diseases, humans (like rabbits) can increase their numbers in *geometric ratios (1-2-4-8-16-etc.)*, whereas the Earth's food production capacity increases only in *arithmetic ratios (1-2-3-4-5-etc.)*. The obvious tendency and possibility is for populations to outstrip food supplies.

Since 1850 to the present, world population has increased more than four-fold—almost exponentially (Figure 1a)—from about 1.5 to 6.5 billion. Growth numbers like these are not easy to assimilate. Another way to try to understand the urgency of these numbers is to divide the world's present population into two halves of 3 billion each. It took over 100,000 years to 1960 for the world's population to reach 3 billion. *The second 3 billion was added in only 39 years and was reached in 1999!*

Paralleling the world's population increase were the "Knowledge Explosion", the "Advancement of the Sciences", the "Proliferation of Technology", and the "Medical Revolution" already mentioned. Figure 1b lists 20 such events and keys them to Figure 1a, the "World Population Growth" curve.

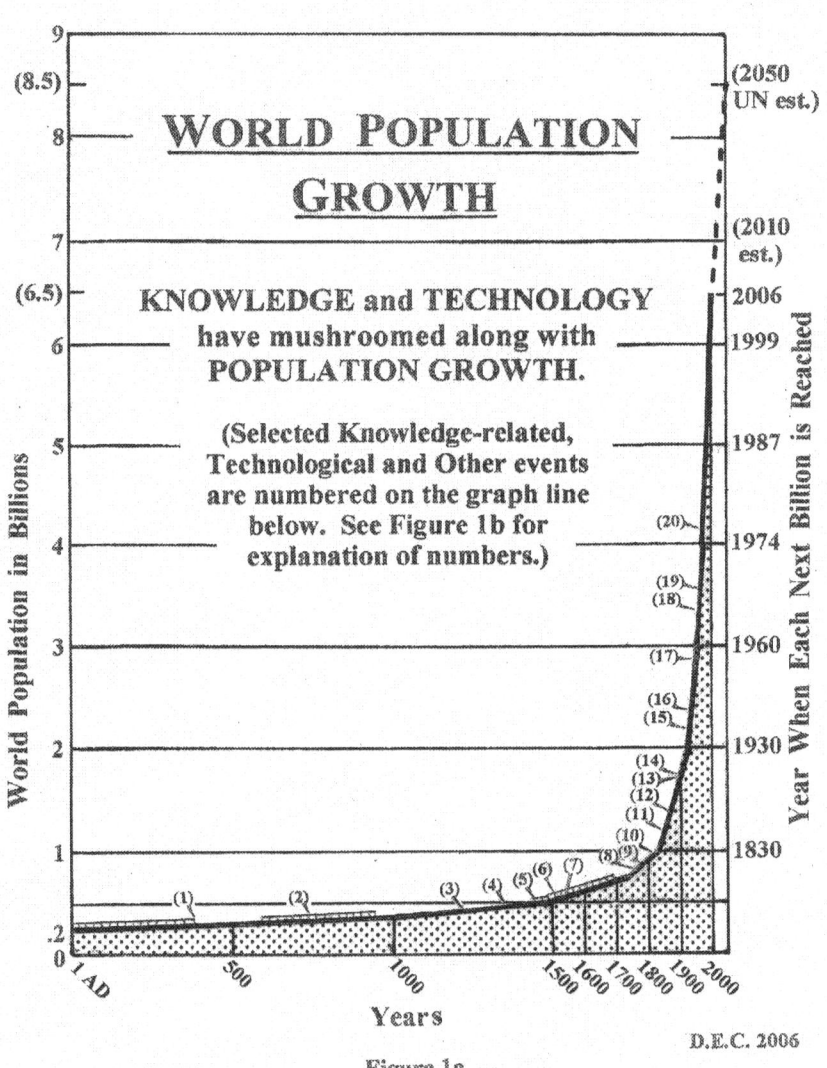

Figure 1a

SELECTED KNOWLEDGE, TECHNOLOGY AND OTHER EVENTS

(Numbers keyed to Figure 1a, "World Population Growth" graph)

(1)   395—End of Roman Empire

(2)   600-950 China—Golden Age of Cultural and Technological Developments

(3)   1215 England—Magna Carta

(4)   Bubonic Plague in Europe

(5)   1455 Germany—Gutenberg Printing Press

(6)   1450-1700—Age of Discovery, European Renaissance

(7)   1543 Poland/Germany—Copernicus' "Heliocentric Theory" (Sun-centered solar system)

(8)   1769 England—Steam Engine Improvements by Watt

(9)   1787: U.S. Constitution, 1789 and 1791: Bill of Rights

(10) Early 1800s England—First Steam-Powered Railroad on flanged tracks

(11) 1850s U.S.—Industrial Scale Steel Production

(12) 1867 England—Lister Introduces Sterilization

(13) 1905 Germany—Einstein's $E = mc2$

(14) 1914–1918 World War I in Europe & League of Nations

(15) 1930s & 1940s U.S.—Beginnings of Computers and Transistors

(16) 1939–1945—War II & United Nations

(17) 1957 USSR—Sputnik in Orbit around Earth

(18) 1960s & 1970s U.S.—Personal Computers & Internet

(19) 1969 U.S.—Man on the Moon

(20) 1970s—World Population and Damage to Natural Systems Increase Beyond Earth's Ability to Maintain All Living Things.

D.E.C.—2006

Figure 1b

Early in the twentieth century the manufacture and adoption of farm machines of all kinds increased agricultural production. However, use of machines also reduced the need for extra "farm hands", especially in the United States. Farmers gave up relatively self-sufficient general farming, and, as was noted, they gave up using horses and raising their own horse feed and became dependant on gasoline to run tractors and electricity to run other machines.

Machines required fewer farm workers and larger farms were more economical, so farm consolidation took place. Economically dispossessed farm families moved to towns and cities to seek work in new factories and services. An expanding network of rails and roads became the economic veins and arteries of our country's economy, connecting farms with markets in the cities. Virtually all farms now depend on gasoline and electricity, but specialty farms then and now depend on seasonal low paid "migrant" workers to help at harvest time.

New agricultural techniques for plant and animal production have increased agricultural production impressively. Advanced techniques have been adopted primarily by industrialized countries, although some areas, like northern India, did well for a few decades after World War II growing improved strains of wheat and rice by adopting "Green Revolution" techniques that required generous use of fertilizers and water. These latter requirements and the purchase of special seeds have put the "Green Revolution" out of reach of most farmers in developing countries.

Biotechnology, a relatively new agricultural technology, develops genetically modified crops to resist certain diseases and increase the yield per acre. It *is* likely to increase agricultural production in the decades ahead. But, with the costs involved and the need to purchase special seeds for every planting, it too will be adopted mostly in countries that already are technologically advanced, and increases in population are likely to counter any gains in world food supply.

Biotechnology also is controversial and has its limits. The controversy surrounds the possible long-term effect on humans of eating genetically modified foods. Also, there must be a photosynthesis limit a (related to soil quality and the input of fertilizers, sunlight and precipitation) on how much plant material can grow on a given piece of land on a sustainable basis that will not compromise the quality of the soil. Further, with the increasing use of farm products and plant residue materials for biofuel production, the problem of maintaining soil fertility becomes a challenging and critical problem.

Perhaps most people have never thought about the Earth's "carrying capacity" for humans but most of us have heard predictions that the Earth could support several times its present population and "not to worry" about population growth. However, regardless of such predictions, Malthus' analysis still is valid even though its proof has been delayed for two centuries by impressive technological advances based largely on fossil fuels and "energy slaves". Even as food production has increased in recent decades, for several decades demands of the human family already have been outstripping the Earth's ability to repair damage to its natural systems. And quite clearly the Earth does not provide adequately for all of the 6.5 billion humans present on a dependable, sustainable basis. Malthus' ideas are alive and well.

A Simplified Lesson on Soils. An adequate supply of food for the Earth's people is not simply a matter of the gross output of agricultural products. Nations vary widely on the quality and amount of their tillable soil. And the quality of soil depends in large part on the environment in which the soil has developed and the care with which it has been farmed. Following are vignettes of three of the world's important but very different kinds of soil.

During the millions of years when living plants and animals were evolving on Earth, **vast areas of grasses** of many types developed and thrived in many places. Middle Illinois was a flowing sea of grasses up to nine feet tall! A key feature of soils that developed under these grassland soils is that they developed in areas where average precipitation was adequate for growth of the grasses *but* was *not* so generous as to leach away the organic residue and mineral salts that accumulate from dead grass. The dead grass residue, accumulating over thousands of years, made natural **grassland soils** several feet thick. These soils are sweet (alkaline), very fertile and black or brown in color. These are the best natural soils in the world for production of grasses, the domestication of which was the basis of raising wheat and barley and the Agricultural Revolution.

In the United States grassland soils are the primary soils of the Great Plains from north Texas to Montana and the Dakotas and from the foothills of the Rocky Mountains east to Missouri, Illinois and Indiana. The eastern portion of this area in the U.S. Midwest is called the "Corn belt". A large part of Argentina and Ukraine also have natural grassland soils, as do a few other places in the world.

With "supplementary irrigation" from ground water sources grassland soils also can produce much more than grain. However, supplementary irrigation can increase the productivity of these areas with excellent soils only as long as ground water is not too expensive to pump from wells that must go deeper and deeper as the water is used faster than it can be replenished by nature. Already some western grassland soil areas, with their economically retrievable ground water supplies having run out, are reverting from raising corn and soybeans to range land and raising wheat.

"Podzolic" (ash-like) **soils** developed under well-watered **forests in mid-latitude areas** in eastern United States, west and central Europe, North China and Japan. These soils tend to be more acidic and usually are not high in natural fertility. However, with crop rotation and organic and other fertilizer materials added, crops of many types can do well on a long-term basis. With careful management, forest soils in Europe, China and Japan have supported large populations for many centuries.

Tropical rain forests are known for their luxuriant growth of trees and other plants. However, the soils in these equatorial areas are very low in natural fertility. The high annual rainfall dissolves and carries organic nutrients from surface layers and deposits these several feet down or is carried away. Thus the typical luxuriant growth in these areas is possible *in spite of* the poor soils. Some plants thrive on the surface leaf mold accumulation. The large trees that provide the spectacular jungle canopy with tangles of vines have deep roots that can tap the deeper deposits of nutrients.

Soils in the abundantly watered tropical rain forests are so poor that these areas have been called "green deserts". Native farming in patches of these forest areas can be productive only for a few years using a system called "shifting cultivation". Then the group must move on and clear other patches for planting. The land abandoned must be left for at least a generation to regenerate before being cleared again for planting.

The March 13, 2006, issue of *Newsweek* carried an unlikely story titled: "Nigeria Could Feed Africa". The story is about the hopeful expectations of "European" farmers being resettled from Zimbabwe's better savanna soils to the edge of Nigeria's tropical rain forest. Even with the best of intentions Nigeria's rain forest soils will not be able to produce on a sustainable basis, and even with the savanna soils in Nigeria's north, certainly could not "Feed Africa"!

The Diverse Issues of Farming. Providing food for humans everywhere on Earth has many facets as well as problems. Eliminating malnutrition and starvation is not a matter of simply providing food to people in need or reducing the population. It also must include setting up agricultural systems in develop-ing countries by which people will raise most of their own food and other farm products. Attention must be given to a balanced diet including vitamins and minerals, fair prices for farm produce and a fair and dependable distribution system for food and fiber already produced. Who owns and controls the land and wages paid to farm workers also are important factors in trying to deal with malnutrition and starvation.

Large scale corporate farming is carried on in many countries. However, the goal is profit for owners and shareholders rather than sustainability, and their practices tend toward depleting and eroding soil, the basic resource of all farm-ing. Agricultural techniques and practices of corporate farms have virtually eliminated "family farming" and "general farming" in the U.S. Imports of cor-porate farm raised food staples have displaced many small subsistence farmers in developing countries.

New agricultural practices themselves, including large scale farming practices, are causing problems that in the years ahead will reduce food production. Agricultural practices that are not sustainable include: heavy use of pesticides and fertilizer—some of which runs off fields and pollutes ground water sources, destruction of habitats for all other forms of life (including a decline in the number of bees and other plant pollinators), lack of adequate fallowing (soil resting), soil erosion, soil depletion of important micro-minerals (that are taken away with the crop and not replaced by fertilizer), and monoculture (large areas raising only one or two crops year after year, making them more susceptible to pests and diseases).

In addition, massive farm machines compact the soil so other machines must be used occasionally to break up the "hardpan" and keep upper soil layers from becoming impervious to necessary water and air percolation. These realities are steadily decreasing the viability and inventory of the Earth's "arable soils". Agricultural specialists in Cuba say it took four or five years after 1991 to reconstitute the soil with organic matter and microorganisms after the big machine/ commercial fertilizer farming methods were replaced.

Other methods of food production also are not sustainable as they are practiced today and will result in less food production in the future. Already mentioned was irrigation farming in high evaporation areas which results in concentra-tions of accumulated salty minerals on and near the surface. And, as was also mentioned, "too efficient" fish trawling and other fish harvesting techniques are threatening the survival of many species that are an important part of our food supply and the nutrition needs of the human family.

The World's "Arable" Lands. My contention that the Earth is overpopulated hinges largely on the Earth's inventory of "arable land" and calculations relating to calories of food consumed by humans. The importance of arable land to human survival cannot be overemphasized. Everything else has little meaning if there is not enough food.

The term "arable land" was introduced a few pages back, as "fertile land" or "tillable, crop raising" land. The term "arable land" therefore is not a precise term and in general means "farmable land" or "land that can be cultivated" to distinguish it from rangeland for livestock and land used for tree crops. Although arable land is considered a "renewable resource", it also is subject to depletion by overuse and loss by erosion or by conversion to other uses, so there can be no simple or absolute answer to the question, "How much arable land is there in the world?" at any one moment in time.

In addition to the terms just mentioned, other terms that have been used interchangeably with the term "arable land" include: "productive land", "cropland", "farmable land", "tilled land" and "grainland". And what about "pasture", "permanent pasture", "woodlots", and "permanent cropland" (fruit and nut trees)? Nations do not report uniformly on the proportion of their land areas that are "arable". Even the World Bank in its annual reports for each nation combines crop and pasture land. And the United States CIA does report each nation's percentage of "arable land", but without a definition.

Are lands that need irrigation "arable"? CIA reports list "irrigated land" separately although its use for crops may not be long term. Egypt may come to mind as a country where irrigation based on the Nile River *has been* sustained for thousands of years. However, the soil enriching deposits of silt that came with the annual flooding of the Nile and made sustained irrigation possible were cut off in 1970 by the completion of the Aswan dam in the river's upper reaches. Some of the silt is released to the lower river, but much of it is now deposited behind the dam in Aswan Lake. Irrigation farming below the dam now requires large fertilizer inputs and is subject to all irrigation farming limitations. Egypt is having difficulty feeding its rapidly increasing population, even with two or three crop seasons each year.

The same "sustainability" question can be raised about land that raises crops using supplementary irrigation in the drier lands of western United States. Crop farming in these areas is only a temporary bonanza. Thus, as productive as they may be with naturally fertile soils and irrigation or supplementary irrigation, these lands cannot be considered "arable" on a long-term basis. "Dry farming" techniques used in Montana since early in the 1900s have not been sustainable because of wind erosion problems.

Arable land is not evenly divided among the world's nations. Citing figures in CIA reports, some countries are well endowed with "arable" land, like Bangladesh with about 62% of its total area considered "arable", Ukraine - 56%, and even the United States with 23%. At the other extreme some countries have far less of their land classified as "arable": Japan 5%, Australia 2%, Canada 4%, Egypt about 3%, and Kuwait less than 1%. Some countries definitely are "have" countries in terms of arable land; others are clearly "have-nots".

However, a high percent of arable land in a country does not guarantee that the people will be fed well or be prosperous. Note Bangladesh with the highest proportion of its land area considered "arable", and yet its people are among the poorest in the world. Near the other extreme are Australia and Canada with small endowments of arable land but with high average levels of living for their relatively small populations. The prosperity of people depends on far more than simply the availability of arable land or population density.

In addition to these agriculture related concerns, the world's inventory of arable land is being steadily reduced by conversion to many other uses. With the growth of population and cities, the farmland around cities, usually some of the best available, is being taken out of production and converted to roads and highways, residential, industrial and other urban uses, airports and shopping malls. Such conversions, made by incremental human decisions as population growth continues, reduce the Earth's capacity to produce food.

Furthermore, as was noted, an increasing amount of arable land is being used to raise crops that are converted to biofuels.

Arable Land Calculations. In the discussion that follows I obviously am pursuing very important questions with data that is imprecise. Nevertheless, the importance of the inquiry overshadows the limited and simplistic data. I use data on the Earth's and the U.S.'s total land area and the percentage of the land area that is arable as reported by the CIA (on the Internet). As was mentioned, no precise definition of the word "arable" is included with the CIA data, which also is unclear whether irrigated land is included or not.

In the Chapter on water I noted that about three-fourths of the Earth's total surface area is covered by oceans and seas; only about one-fourth of the Earth's total area is "land". According to the CIA only 13 per cent of the Earth's land (about 4 3/4 billion acres) is considered "arable". Another study, by Constanza in the May 1997 issue of *Nature*, reports that only 9% of the Earth's land is classed as "cropland". Perhaps the larger CIA figure reflects the inclusion of irrigated land.

A CIA report states that during the last 8 years the world's inventory of arable land has increased. How can that be with population increases and constant conversions to other uses? That increase has come mostly from large-scale clearing and converting tropical rain forests to pasture, much of which is used to raise cattle products for export to the U.S. However, considering the organic limits of tropical rain forest soils that were described and using my definition (next paragraph) it should be clear that tropical rain forest lands used for pasture are not truly "arable" on a sustainable basis. In a relatively short time these "pasture lands" will have to revert to tropical rain forests. In contrast to the CIA report, a National Geographic map, "A World Transformed" published in 2002, asserts: "Degraded soils have lowered global yields by 13 percent since World War II", even as the population is increasing!

With these somewhat contradictory and wide-ranging considerations and for lack of a precise definition, I use the following: *"Arable land is farmland which, with good management and with no supplementary water inputs, can raise crops on a sustainable basis."* Even as I write that definition, I realize that climate change also is likely to modify "water inputs" and thus change the arable (or not) status of soils in some areas.

Decades ago it was calculated that 2.5 acres of arable land was needed to supply the food and fiber to support a person at an average U.S. level of living. New agricultural techniques, pesticides and herbicides have greatly increased yield and production per acre and reduced that figure. Calculations reveal that in 2006 for each person in the United States there are 1.2 acres of arable land. Among the nations of the world we are among the most fortunate in our arable land endowment, but all is *not* well if one considers the well-being of everyone living in the U.S. We have more food wastage than others and at least

10% of our citizens (30+ million!), including many children, still live below the poverty line and do not get adequate nutrition.

In contrast to the U.S., the picture for the world as a whole is grim. With 6.5 billion people and 4.75 billion acres of arable land in the world, it is clear there is far less than one acre available per person to provide food and fiber. Using the CIA data there is only .73 acre of arable land per person available. Using the less generous Constanza data, .62 acres of arable land is available per person. If one sets the U.S., Ukraine and Argentina and a few other countries that are well—endowed with arable land aside from a world calculation, only about .6 and .5 acres of arable land is available per person. This means that, unless a country is a significant food importer, most of the people are in jeopardy of malnutrition or starvation.

About 1 billion of our fellow humans never get enough to eat; they are starving or close to it and many of them live in Sub-Saharan Africa. Some say there would be no starvation problem in the world IF there were a better distribution system of food now produced, or IF more productive techniques were used, or IF small loans at reasonable rates were available in developing countries. Those "IFs" are interesting and could be encouraging from a theoretical point of view, but there is little movement to adopt such measures worldwide to convert those "IFs" to reality at any time soon.

It is now generally accepted that an average of 1 acre (.4 hectare) of arable land is needed to supply the 2300 to 2400 calories required per person for healthy living. We also know from the calculations noted above that even now there is significantly less than .73 or .62 acres of arable land per person for most people in the world. Therefore, regardless of the theoretical "IFs" mentioned, the amount of arable land available per person in the world is not enough *now* to provide, at a reasonable level of living, the food and fiber needs of the 6.5 billion in our huge human family. Furthermore, these calculations do not consider the food and fiber needs of the 120 million additions each year to the world's population. These calculations also do not consider arable land *losses* to accommodate additional people (urban expansions, etc.), the expected disruptions to arable land and agricultural productivity by climate change, etc.

Calories and Food Supply. Another way to judge the adequacy (or inadequacy) of world food production and confirm the overpopulation crisis is to calculate—even roughly—the calories needed to support the world's *present* population at *current nutrition levels* that include a billion people who are at or near starvation.

The same caloric approach can then be used to calculate the caloric needs to provide an *adequate diet* for all of the world's present population.

Considering individuals of all ages, sizes and activity levels, there is consensus among nutritionists that an average of 2300 to 2400 calories per person is needed per day to maintain reasonable health. It also seems to be agreed that those who receive less than 2000 calories per day are hungry, malnourished, subject to more infections and diseases, and are less able to work or think effectively.

In Table 1 below, most of the "General Nutrition Levels" [shown in Column A] represent areas of the world with different levels of living areas and different average levels of calorie intake in their diet. The purpose of Table 1 is to calculate estimates of the *total calories* now consumed by individuals at different levels of nutrition [*bottom of Col B3*], and compare this number with the calories that would be needed to provide all of the world's 6.5 billion individuals with a reasonable diet [bottom of Col. C6].

To make this comparison, Column B-1 divides the present world population into very general nutrition cohorts (people grouped by some characteristic) relating to the caloric intake areas represented in Column A. Column B-2 shows the average daily per capita caloric intake for each cohort. By multiplying Columns B-1 and 2 for each cohort, Column B-3 shows each cohort's total daily caloric need in trillions of calories, with the total at the bottom.

Column C-4 represents the present world population divided into nutrition cohorts with all persons at an Intermediate level of caloric intake or higher. By multiplying Columns C-4 and 5 for each cohort, Column C-6 shows each cohort's total daily caloric need in trillions of calories, again with the total at the bottom.

Columns 1, 2 and 3 present the estimated "bottom line reality" that the human family now consumes roughly 15.0 trillion calories per day. The last two cohorts in Col. A ("Devlpg. Nations" and "Hunger") represent the reality that at least 2 billion of our neighbors on this planet are malnourished, with daily diets less than 2000 calories per day, and of these nearly 1 billion are in chronic hunger, most of them in Africa struggling to survive on about 1300 calories per day.

Columns 4, 5, and 6 show that to provide all 6.5 billion members of the human family with an adequate diet, would require about 17.3 trillion calories per day, 2.3 trillion calories more than is presently available, a 13% deficit, and these calculations *do not* take into consideration that world population is steadily increasing.

Table 1: COMPARING WORLD CALORIC NEEDS

A General Nutrition Levels	B Present World Nutrition Levels			C Everyone With Adequate Nutrition		
	1	2	3	4	5	6
	2006 Population (billions)	Per/cap Caloric Intake (cals/day)	Col. 1 x Col. 2 (trillions of cals/day)	2006 Population (billions)	Per/cap Caloric Intake (cals/day)	Col. 4 x Col. 5 (trillions of cals/day)
"N.Am. diet"	1.5	3000	4.5	1.5	3000	4.5
"Euro. diet"	1	2600	2.6	4	2600	10.4
"Intermed."	2	2400	4.8	1	2400	2.4
"Devlpg. Nations"	1	1800	1.8			
"Hunger"	1	1300	1.3			
TOTAL	6.5		15.0	6.5		17.3

There are contingencies that could alter these generalities. Elimination of food waste and more intelligent eating in affluent countries (especially the United States!) and elimination of rodent losses in poorer countries might make about 1 trillion more calories available.

However, these additions will be counterbalanced by arable land losses to production by the conversions that have been mentioned (expansion of urban uses to accommodate more people, erosion, overuse, depletion of ground water supplies, salinization, and by returning to forest some lands better suited to that use on a sustainable basis). Further (and again), these estimates do not consider the largely unknowable negative impacts of global warming on food production or the world's steady population increase.

Nutrition, Fish and Omega 3 Fatty Acids. Assessing adequate human nutrition involves much more than calculations of arable land and caloric intake. Our food must include a variety of particular proteins, fiber, vitamins and minerals (some in "micro" amounts) and other inputs, like Omega 3 fatty acids from fish, that research suggests are important for brain function.

As was noted, the world's fisheries are about 90% depleted of varieties of fish products most sought, and most of this depletion has taken place since World War II with use of too efficient driftnet equipment and sonar. With the collapse of local fish stocks, the problem has been exacerbated by government subsidies of fishermen to obtain larger boats that can range farther in their search for a livelihood.

Summary of Arable Land and Calorie Considerations. The Universal Declaration of Human Rights, which was passed unanimously by the U.N. General Assembly in December 1948, states that: "Every human being has the right to be free from hunger; the right to adequate food; the right to clean, safe drinking water". The document makes no mention how these rights are to be fulfilled, but they are among the "Millennium Goals" of the U.N. for the year 2015.

Conclusions drawn from the arable land calculations and Table 1 above indicate that, using present economic systems and agricultural technologies, the world does not fulfill for the Earth's *present* 6.5 billions of humans the basic right to have an adequate diet and to be "free from hunger". Estimates by the Zero Population Growth organization are that in 1985 the Earth could support 6 billion humans on an adequate vegetarian diet, 4 billion on a diet with 15% of animal product calories, and only 2.5 with a 35% animal products diet (This and other important food and population information is on the Internet under "zpg 20").

Regardless of the "buts", "what ifs" and "maybes", if we are not providing adequately for those who are here now, what will happen to the 120 million who are added each year and the billions who will be born in coming years? Population pressures already are reducing the Earth's food productivity. If we do little or nothing even more people will be starving and malnourished than our two billion neighbors on the planet who *at present* are not getting enough to eat! We will be breeding massive unrest and increased terrorism.

The Imminent Global Food Crisis. It is true that the human animal, with its violent competitiveness for the Earth's limited resources, could go along with things getting steadily worse for decades. It is true that at a minimal or bare subsistence level of living for all people the Earth (theoretically) could support several times its present 6.5 billion humans—but that also could be done *only for a few decades*.

Why for only a few decades? By either of these scenarios, if we continue to permit the growth of the Earth's population we will see a further breakdown in the Earth's ecosystems that support all living things, with catastrophic results. By pressures for more and more production the availability and productivity of our arable lands will decline still further, our massive cities will become even more unlivable, fresh water will become like gold, and global warming will disrupt just about everything.

Figure 2 demonstrates this difficult situation. The *solid curved* line represents how world population has increased from 1700 to 2006. It is estimated by several calculations that in 1970 when world population was 4 billion the number of humans passed the "Earth's Carrying Capacity for Humans".

Since the 1970s billions more humans have put increasing demands on the world's limited fresh water supplies and caused a steady deterioration in the Earth's ecosystems, including the inventory of arable land. With the large proportion of the world's human population under the age of fifteen, population gains will continue for decades, *even with* intensive family planning and birth control education and programs that might be put in place in the next few years.

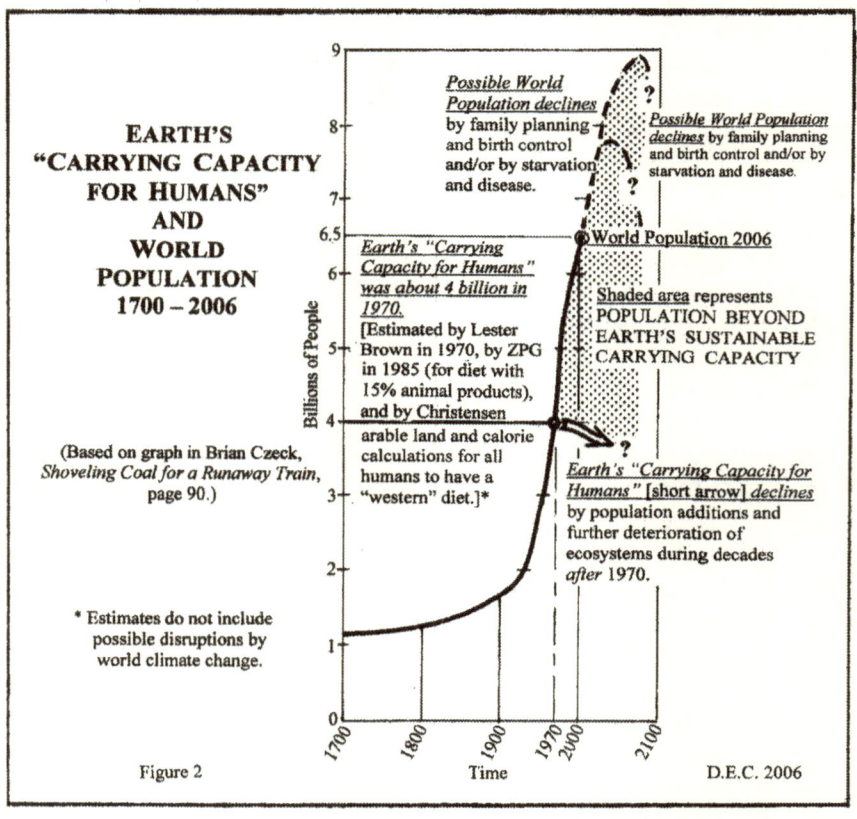

Figure 2

With these considerations in mind, Figure 2 shows as *dashed lines* the possibilities for further world population gain and then decline later this century. The sharp declines seen as a possibility by demographers will come—finally—as a result of far fewer births and/or deaths from massive starvation and disease.

The *shaded area* in Figure 2 represents population growth *beyond Earth's Carrying Capacity* for humans since 1970. Furthermore, following the decades of continuing ecosystem deterioration by increases in the human family, the Earth's *capacity to support humans* also would have declined, as suggested by the *arrow dropping below the 4 billion level* for world population. The longer we wait to take action to reduce birth rates and family size, the Earth's ability to support the human family on a sustainable (forever) basis will steadily decline.

We must not tinker with small changes to continue "business as usual". By using our brains and applying the compassion that is in each of us, we can make the changes in our attitudes, values and actions (especially in regard to family planning and birth control) and emerge from the difficult decades ahead as a stabilized and then a smaller human family, a human family the Earth can sustain, but a human family that will be more caring and sharing of the Earth's bounty and, having abandoned war, will be at peace.

We MUST take the positive road, and the sooner the better! We do not want to leave our grandchildren and those who will follow with a dismal prospect for their lives.

The United States' Favored Position. Looking at the world as a whole, American citizens live in an "oasis". Our country is one of the most favored in the world in terms of its food producing capability. The United States has four kinds of reserve for its food producing future.

First, the U.S. exports far more corn and wheat than any other nation, so we could discontinue exporting large quantities of grain and use it to feed people in the United States. Of course if we were to do that there would be enormous negative consequences in many countries, including China, that depend on our exports. **Second**, we could shift our diets to include less meat, and save at least part of the 16 to 1 feed conversion loss that is a reality in raising animals for food, rather than eating vegetation materials directly. However, a significant shift to more vegetarian diets would completely upset the "livestock industry". **Third**, we could eliminate various agricultural programs that have paid farmers to leave some of their land idle.

The U.S. also has a **fourth** kind of "reserve". If, after making the tough adjustments mentioned above, the people in the United States faced the need to produce still more food, all over the country there are additional sources of "arable land". Large and small patches of lawns around our homes and estates, open spaces in parks, golf courses, vacant lots in towns and cities, and even rooftops, all could be converted into "urban gardens". We could learn from Cuba where, since the early 1990s, such stringent measures have been taken to raise enough food for the people. However, now comes the negative side: With population gains, further losses and deterioration of our arable land, and biofuel competition, even taking advantage of these four kinds of "reserve" would continue our "favored position" for only a few decades.

The United States simply cannot continue as an oasis of prosperity in the world with increasing poverty and starvation. If we were to try to turn our backs on the rest of the world we would have to make our country an *isolationist fortress* and give up many attributes of our "comfortable" way of life. Our democracy would vanish as we traded our popular government for more security (as Athens did). Anything we did or tried to do elsewhere in the world would be the target of constant intense terrorism. Tourism and safe travel and dependable trade would be impossible.

The only viable solution is for the United States to acknowledge that all countries and people are interdependent. We depend on the rest of the world for many things that support our high-tech, affluent (and wasteful) way of life. And other countries depend on the United States for food and other important items. Without many special products from elsewhere in the world life in the US would revert to activities, technologies and products of a century ago.

Even at a more modest level of living those living in the U.S. cannot (and should not try to) get along alone. We cannot continue indefinitely our critical and costly imports and our deepening indebtedness to banks and countries overseas. A day of financial reckoning surely will come.

As intelligent and caring creatures, where is our conscience and our religion? These should be urging each of us to really help those who are less well off and to modify our wasteful and unsustainable ways. At some level of our thinking we must admit that world poverty is a major taproot of terrorism. We cannot fight terrorism with the military. Why can't we accept realities so evident around us?

Some of those who brush off the overpopulation issue say that the human future is not limited by the arable lands on which we depend today. They are counting on using a much larger portion of the Earth's land to produce food by yet-to-be-developed technologies, an argument negated by the Ehrlichs in 1990. They overlook the Earth's critical fresh water issue. They do not take into account all of the inputs needed to develop and retain soil productivity. They ignore the continuing elimination of habitat for the countless other species with whom we share this planet and on whom the Earth's ecological system depends. And they do not consider the unknowns of climate change.

As the few examples presented indicate, many countries do not have enough arable land to provide an adequate diet for their people even now. Some are fortunate and have economies that make importing needed food possible. Others can supplement their land-grown food from marine sources. Many others to not have those options and already are deep in poverty and even starvation.

Many developing countries, especially in Africa, are likely to experience starvation, unrest and perhaps revolution in the decades ahead unless major changes are made in government, land ownership and distribution of wealth. Add to those problems the AIDS pandemic south of the Sahara, and it is easy to understand that village systems for security and food production are being decimated.

Because of several poor harvest years and overdrawing water, especially in North China, it was mentioned that China already is importing large amounts of grain, and must import even more in the years ahead. India, with many hungry people and increasing population will need more food. Despite more productive new strains of rice, the India's Ganges River waters are being heavily overdrawn and prospects for significant increase in food production are not great.

None of the ominous notes in the paragraphs above take into account the dislocations and disruptions of food production that global climate change will bring on. The title of Al Gore's book and movie, *An Inconvenient Truth*, actually understates the enormity of that "truth". When that "truth" arrives it will be far more than simply "inconvenient"; it will be devastating and will disrupt civilization as we know it!

Food Solutions? An Alternet article citing a recent Oxford University study notes that ocean fish may obtain Omega 3 fatty acids from some special strains of algae that "probably" can be produced commercially (<http://www.alternet.org/module/printversion/37862>). If this is so, raising these algae for human food directly or as food for fish in fish farms might help overcome the cognitive-related deficiency that is caused by an Omega 3 fatty acid deficiency. Fish products now used in pet foods and fertilizer also could be diverted to food for humans. However, unless the fish were fed the special strain of algae, they would not produce the Omega 3 fatty acids needed by humans.

Hydroponics (food plants raised intensively indoors in fertilizer enriched water) could augment food supplies, however this is a labor intensive process, requires special inputs, and is useful on a small scale only in special circumstances (as on spaceships). Hydroponics does not offer hope for feeding the billions of humans who are here or on their way.

The United States and other developed nations could help "developing nations" to adopt farming methods that would help the people in those areas be less dependant on imported foods. By encouraging dispersed land ownership, food self-sufficiency, and application of agricultural technology adapted to small farms in developing nations, the common people in those areas would benefit and their increased prosperity could make them customers for other goods from "developed nations". However, multi-national agricultural and industrial corporations and the financial institutions that profit from projects that benefit only a small portion of people in those developing countries would oppose such changes.

There is no question that soil, the Earth's "skin", is a precious "renewable resource". Regardless of culture or religion, farms and farming must be managed wisely so the soil will remain available for the next and all generations. It was noted that monoculture actually "mines" the soil by not replacing all nutrients that are removed with the harvested crop. This will become an even greater problem when more crop residues are used for biofuels. Actual soil renewal takes many decades of organic material growing and dying in place for the "residues" to form an inch of useful soil.

As for adequacy of basic materials from which common fertilizer materials are made, nitrogen fertilizers draw that element from the atmosphere, a virtually unlimited supply. Two other fertilizer materials, phosphate and potash, come from nature, and both are one-time-use "exhaustible resources". However, there are ample reserves of these materials around the world for now, and I emphasize the "for now". The U.S. has adequate reserves of phosphate but very little potash, underscoring again our dependence on other countries for a critical import.

Increasing use of fertilizers has been responsible for increases in production of most agricultural crops in the last several decades, but a practical limit has been reached. Adding still more fertilizer to fields results in only small "non-economic" gains in crop yield per acre.

Every person must see himself or herself as a temporary resident of the Earth and a steward of its bounty. Where is it written that for the long term success of the human experiment on Earth individuals would have the right to ruin a part of the ecosystem for their short-term gain? I remember a cartoon in which a farmer commented to his neighbor that he now owned the farm, but that it cost him 15 years and 6 inches of topsoil. Although this was a cartoon, it no doubt has happened and is happening! With similar mismanagement, after a few changes in ownership the topsoil on those farms would be gone!

Farming that "mines the soil" is not stewardship and should be illegal! It ignores all responsibility for future generations. As more and more people crowd the Earth more pressure will be put on our arable land to increase food production with devastating long-term consequences that could break down the whole system. Natural processes cannot keep up with the degradation and erosion that is taking place now. The only intelligent and long term answer is for world population to stabilize and then decrease.

So Can Anything Be Done? Again here are more "*Fs*". *IF* waste could be eliminated from food use in wealthier countries, *IF* food losses from rodents and poor storage could be sharply reduced everywhere but especially in developing countries, *IF* large and small scale farmers and factory farm managers would adopt sustainable techniques to all of the world's arable land, *IF* multi-national agribusiness corporations and financial institutions would modify their colonial-like policies of domination and help the world's poor people, *IF* food financing, storage and delivery systems could be arranged to help those in need, and *IF* global warming was not happening, then perhaps in a few years the world's current population of 6.5 billion people could be adequately fed at a daily average of 2400 calories for a few years. But those *IFs*, certainly in their totality, do not represent reality.

There is wastage! Global warming is happening! And multi-national corporations are not likely to morph into "do good" organizations. Furthermore, what about the added billions of people who will be here before any actions we might take today have a chance to take effect? Overpopulation is a serious challenge NOW!

In his seminal book, *Plan B 2.0*, Lester Brown suggests that in the production of everything for human use from the Earth's offerings, the costs assigned at various stages in their production and manufacture should include repair of negative environmental consequences of that production. In doing so we would not be "taking the Earth for granted" and would be providing funds for "repairing" and restoring the Earth to maintain and sustain our use of its bounty. The added costs to final products surely will affect what is produced, its cost, and choices made by consumers.

Brown's idea of including in the cost of every item the cost of its environmental impacts therefore is not a "pie in the sky" idea; it is sound long-term economics. For too long humans have been able to use resources in a particular area, and move on with no responsibility for maintaining the environment as it was. The "moving on" age is over. Humans have always ignored "Earth costs" in their economic calculations. We are being forced to repair centuries of misuse and neglect of our Earth home, or else.

Conclusion. The conclusion of this chapter is that the human animal has acted as if the Earth's offerings are unlimited and that the Earth would always renew itself. We have acted as if there would always be enough arable land and fresh water. We have reproduced our kind as if the Earth could support an unlimited number of humans. We must understand that those days are gone for many reasons. The human family already is using up the Earth's productive base.

We ARE in a time of judgment, but the time and the reasons we are here are of our own making. And we have a choice: Should we carry on blindly as we have been doing and watch our so-called civilization collapse around us like a house of cards?

Or as intelligent creatures, can we abandon our violent, wasteful war-making propensity and work with our neighbors on this planet through a Limited Global Government to address the converging crises? The bottom line is: We must halt the growth of the world's population and reduce the human family so a long term sustainable relationship with our Earth home can be established.

It is up to us.

CHAPTER 4

BUILDING MATERIALS

In terms of an individual's needs, providing shelter does not have the same immediacy for survival as air, water, food and even clothing. Humans are a hardy lot and they can become accustomed to unusual cold and heat.

Virtually every part of the world offers materials for shelters and different kinds of structures, whether those shelters and structures are caves, tents, or are made with stone, clay, lumber or thatch. There was no shortage of these materials in the past and there is none now, although not all materials are available everywhere. In this brief chapter I will focus on materials for "shelter", an obvious human need.

Since earliest times forests have provided materials for shelter, however availability varies widely. Petrified logs confirm that a long time ago trees were common in the Sahara and many other areas now deserts. In Europe forests were cut-over to facilitate farming and settlements. In the United States large scale forest cutting took place throughout the1800s and early 1900s. In recent decades equatorial tropical rain forests are being cutover rapidly, with much of the cleared land used to establish pastures to raise beef for export.

Besides producing various wood products for humans, forests have other important functions in nature. Their roots stabilize the soils on hills and mountainsides. They moderate the spring and summer release of meltwater from alpine snow packs. Trees need and use carbon dioxide in the atmosphere and convert it to oxygen. Forests support many plants and animals that are part of the Earth's genome inventory. We need to use and maintain forests carefully.

We live in a world of "shelter extremes", not only in climatic terms. At one extreme and as noted in an Ann Landers quote in my *Healing the World,* eighty percent of the world's people live in substandard housing. Too many of our fellow world citizens live in mud huts and shantytowns without electricity, plumbing, etc. Even in the United States some are homeless, in poverty, and live on the streets or in crowded squalor.

At the other extreme, wealthier individuals and families in rich and poor countries maintain two or more residences in different parts of their country or elsewhere in the world. Another example of the "shelter gap" is evident in the United States in recent decades, where the average size and cost of new "single-family" homes is more than double what is used to be. This probably temporary trend toward enormous sized "homes"—larger than the "inns" of past generations—is occurring even as the size of families occupying these huge homes has decreased.

With the Industrial Revolution, unemployed folk from the countryside were pushed from the farms to seek work in large and small cities and towns in developed countries, leaving rural villages struggling to survive.

In developing countries opportunities in cities also have drawn people in from rural areas. Many of the larger cities in developing countries have European-like downtowns and elegant walled or gated residential neighborhoods. These neighborhoods are peopled by a new but small middle class that is supported by businesses and industries from industrialized nations. Many of these same cities in developing countries also are ringed by shanty-towns, filled with country people who, having left their villages of thatched huts, struggle to make a living by the "informal" economic sector. Shanty-towns consist largely of "build-it-yourself shelters", but in many no basic water, sewage or electric services are provided to these crowded neighborhoods by the government.

Most homes in developed nations and those in better-off neighborhoods in developing nations now include as "necessities" such items as flush toilets, telephones, cell phones, computers with world-embracing Internet connections, and perhaps even a FAX connection.

In industrialized countries new and "improved" construction materials have been developed and are transported long distances. Local materials may have been used up and it is common practice now to use the new synthetic materials, some designed to "copy" natural materials. Most of these new materials require much energy in their manufacture, and many are made in part from petroleum, the basic fossil fuel. New materials like plastic or plywood may be stronger or more weather resistant than natural materials, but some of these materials have a lingering "offgas" problem that can impinge negatively on the health of individuals.

In thinking about housing issues in the United States, hurricane Katrina's August 2005 wipeout of largely black neighborhoods in New Orleans comes to mind. Katrina, in all of its unhealthy racial, economic and government aspects, revealed the sorry underbelly of the powerful and world-dominating United States. Over a year after Katrina, hundreds of thousands of New Orleans' residents are still without permanent homes.

By the nature of its location, New Orleans will be built back to take its place near the mouth of the Mississippi River as a significant port city, but its population may be significantly smaller. Its low-lying areas should be left to absorb future water surges; they should *not* be rebuilt as residential neighborhoods. Citizens from those flooded areas, when (and if) they return to New Orleans, should be assisted to live on higher ground elsewhere in the city. Levees should *not* be rebuilt higher and then higher to try to contain more great hurricanes that surely will come.

Questions can also be raised about large federal government housing projects that in decades past were built in many cities for those with lower incomes. As well intended as those projects were to fulfill the "right to shelter", they did not fulfill the expectations of a better life for those who moved in. Instead, because poverty itself was not addressed, some of these projects degenerated into gang and drug dealing havens. Some of these, like the Pruitt-Igoe project in St. Louis, were built and have been demolished at government (taxpayer) expense. A lesson can be learned from these projects and demolitions: Economic development and the elimination of poverty must go along with any project to improve the living conditions and lives of poorer people.

Solutions. In terms of the adequacy of materials like clay, sand, and stone for building, there is no worldwide shortage, regardless of the population growth. However, there are two other kinds of problems.

One involves forests. For a tree to grow to a useful size may take from a dozen to hundreds of years, so the concept of forests being a "renewable resource" needs to be understood with that time interval in mind.

Furthermore, when we remove any product from the land, be it food, fiber or wood, as much of the residue as possible from the harvesting should be left in place to replace the micro-minerals that were essential for the growth of that item and will be needed for the growth of the next. Therefore forests are a renewable resource that can be sustained only with that time caveat and with proper management.

And **secondly**, there are the social problems of homelessness, shanty-towns, slums, racism and people "left behind". These issues do not stem from shortages in the supply of materials for providing shelter. They are problems of economic systems, prejudice and the priorities of distribution and services within countries. Most of these problems relate to the pervasiveness of poverty. With political will and following through on the compassion of their religious beliefs, politicized shelter problems could be resolved to fulfill everyone's "right" to basic housing and a better life.

Among his other accomplishments and inventions, Buckminster Fuller is well known for the "shelter solution" he invented. One of "Bucky" Fuller's key ideas was "to do more with less" in the use of the Earth's resources. He spent his life in dogged efforts to educate the public to use all resources intelligently, including building materials. The "Geodesic Dome" was one of his inventions. Geodesic Domes are inexpensive and efficient hemispherical structures that can be built for many purposes. They can be built small, the size of a small home (and be put in place by helicopter anywhere), or large, such as the 250 foot diameter, 200 foot high "United States Pavilion" at the Montreal "Expo '67" Worlds Fair. For several years "Bucky" Fuller was on the faculty of the Southern Illinois University and lived in Carbondale, Illinois, in a "Geodesic Dome" home that is now on the list of National Historic Buildings.

Another shelter question involves many cities across the United States, like New Orleans, where neighborhoods or structures have been built in flood-prone areas. It is too easy for local governments to grant permission to local developers who are always at their doors wanting to build something, even in areas that should be left in their natural condition. Developers argue that such projects will provide jobs and homes or business structures. The argument, repeated by Chambers of Commerce, has always been that the "highest and best use of any property is that which will generate tax revenue for the government and the most profit" for the owner. It is hard to win favor for reserving land for flood control or for public projects such as parks and bikeways. Attitudes and laws must be changed regarding the need for public projects that make a community more attractive and livable. And "eminent domain" must not be used to take property from one citizen and make it available to another citizen.

For properties in flood prone areas we also hear "Why should we worry about a 100 year flood or a 500 year flood?", especially if the area had a "100 year flood" just a few years earlier. Potential customers of such properties should be educated about what "probabilities" mean. Kaskaskia Island, in the Mississippi River between Illinois and Missouri, experienced two "500 year floods" in the spring and summer of 1993, twice inundating Kaskaskia Island and the remnants of its pioneer village and church.

Federal or other public flood insurance protection should not be granted to those who build in flood-prone areas. Further, if, against the advice and recommendation of environmental and civic experts, individuals choose to build in hazardous areas, taxpayer money should not be used to protect or replace their assets. Hazardous areas would include flood prone areas, beaches subject to hurricanes and storm erosion, federal forest areas subject to natural fires, and no doubt other kinds of areas.

Following Lester Brown's "all costs included" proposal, other approaches to consider in the struggle to balance the People-Earth Equation include: Environment impact costs should be added as "separation taxes" for production from mines and forests. All construction, packing and packaging materials should ultimately be biodegradable.

My conclusion to this chapter is that, unlike water and arable land, the Earth is made of many materials that can be used, and some reused, for building purposes. As for forests and wood products, considering the important ecological functions of forests and their slow renewability, their careful use and management are critical and very relevant to the overpopulation issue.

With issues of jobs and costs that go to the heart of virtually all of our institutions, it will be very difficult to bring to a level of "sustainability" the many complicated and interrelated aspects of the People/Earth Equation. However, we are not lemmings. For our survival and a better future for our children and grandchildren we must try. In my view, an informed and revived political will and a Limited Global Government would give us the best chance.

CHAPTER 5

ENERGY—"ENERGY SLAVES"

The concept of "human resources" was brought up in the Introduction. I noted that human resources include the human abilities to think, to reason, to work, to feel emotions, to be able to remember, and to produce more humans. Note that all of these attributes except the last are "the *ability* to do something".

The *ability* or *potential ability* to think or work, etc. can be used well or poorly or not developed at all. Education and good health obviously are critical in our development and use of human resources. A "human resource", therefore, is not the *product* of thinking or work because all thoughts, skills and the products of work involve that individual's culture. To think, to work, and the other human abilities use energy we gain by eating, sleeping, et cetera. And that is where *energy* comes in as an essential in all human affairs.

However, this chapter is not about human muscle and other powers. This chapter is about the kinds of energy humans have learned to use to *increase their muscle and brain power* and to make more effective and powerful their innate abilities to think, to work, etc. This chapter also is about the sources and supply of the inanimate energy we use.

A graph that showed the increase in human and supplementary energy use through time would show a line very similar to the population increase line shown in Figure 1a, sloping up very gently from earliest times until the last two centuries when, rather quickly, it would become almost vertical.

The more energy we have learned to use, the more advanced we have become in our technology and knowledge about everything. With these a significant but small portion of the human family has attained a comfortable living.

However, even with these gains even greater numbers of our neighbors on this planet have been "left behind". Further, during this century and a half, through new medical science technology the human family has multiplied in numbers over four times!

Our phenomenal advances in the physical sciences and technology—helped greatly by our increasing use of relatively inexpensive fossil fuel energy—have far outstripped our advances in the social sciences. There have been encouraging advances in democracy around the world and the development of international organizations and the U.N. over the last century and a half. But there have been even greater investments of human brain and muscle power and money on the ever-increasing demand by our market economy for constant growth, for more and more consumer products, and for the dead-end support of war preparations and wars which consume and waste much and solve no problems.

Energy Use from Beginnings to Now. When our earliest forebears had separated from the rest of the animal kingdom in the Earth's evolutionary saga, their only attributes were their ability to do things with their muscles and larger brains. Their activities, like the activities of all living creatures, used energy gained through eating things that had been alive. Slowly through language and memory power, humans accumulated insights and skills that made it possible to harness other energy sources. With written language eons later they could pass their increasing knowledge on to subsequent generations. Knowledge became cumulative and "education" of each generation became critical.

As with almost all animals in this early time, the daily life and work of humans was tied to "daylight hours" until the use of fire was discovered and torches, fat lamps and candles were invented. However, even with these innovations little work was done after sunset.

The harnessing of fire was critical in extending the human range of living places to colder environments and to improving the human diet. The domestication of some kinds of animals to do work expanded the energy that was available to fulfill human needs. In contrast to other living things that are limited to a particular ecological niche, the use of fire and animal skins for clothing also made it possible to establish permanent settlements in colder areas.

Through the long train of human history until the Industrial Revolution, all people and cultures were on a fairly level "playing field" in terms of energy use. Walking was the common mode of transportation and the use of domesticated animals, fire, wind and waterpower were nearly universal and reasonably equal across all cultures. Most people were farmers and farms everywhere raised a variety of plant and animal products for farm use with some for sale. And that is about how matters remained until the Industrial Revolution blossomed in Western Europe and the United States in the 1800s.

Buckminster Fuller, mentioned earlier, introduced the term "energy slaves" to connote expansions of work ability and energy use beyond human muscles by wind, water, domesticated animals and machines.

The Industrial Revolution and the advancements in transportation, agricultural and industrial technology that came along have all been possible because of the use of "fossil fuels", which are, in effect, solar energy that has been stored deep in the Earth in the form of coal, petroleum and natural gas since the Carboniferous Age hundreds of millions of years ago. The Industrial Revolution "took off" in the early 1800s with the development of new ways to use coal. With fossil fuels available, humans suddenly multiplied many times over the "energy slaves" at their command.

All modes of transport changed to use fossil fuels. Farmers no longer used horses and gave up raising hay and grain for horse feed and have become dependant on fossil fuels (and electricity generated from fossil fuels) to run their machines. Coal-driven railroads became commonplace and replaced stagecoaches and the pony express. And, more than coincidentally, human slavery has been (almost) discontinued.

From the mid-1800s to the First World War, shifts to fossil fuels changed manufacturing from small craft shops to factories and started migrations of displaced rural folk to the enlarging cities. Many seeking a better life came from Europe to the United States in waves of migration by the millions. With energy slaves from fossil fuels, Western Europe and the United States surged ahead and have continued to dominate the rest of the world for the last two centuries.

By far the greatest use of coal, petroleum and natural gas, all of them "one-time-use" resources, has been as energy to operate motor vehicles and to heat, light and cool our buildings. Only a small portion of fossil fuel use is based on their chemical attributes to produce a wide range of consumer and industrial products.

Energy Problems of Our Time. A bright spot on the bottom of the satellite photo on the cover of *Healing the World* depicts one type of energy waste very clearly. There is a flare of light at the corner of West Africa where the coast turns south. That large lighted spot on Nigeria's coast does not represent a major city, as similar lighted spots do in the twilight and night-shaded parts of Europe. The white blotches at the "Bight of Benin", which are obviously visible from space, represent gas flares burning off natural gas and the electric lighting for 24 hour production from Nigeria's rich delta and coastal oil fields. Many of us have driven past an oil field or oil refinery, especially at night, and seen lighted gas flares. Natural gas is associated with liquid petroleum in the Earth, it is explosive and dangerous, and is burned off as a simple way to get rid of it as part of the liquid petroleum production process. However, burning it off represents the waste of a limited resource that is becoming much more costly in these early years of the twenty-first century. And there now are ways to compress it so it can be shipped to markets.

With investments from multinational petrol corporations, Nigeria has become the world's fifth greatest producer and exporter of petroleum. However, the common people of Nigeria (and some other oil producing countries) have seen little improvement in their level of living. The development of Nigeria's petroleum resource has led to serious unrest and even sabotage involving the delta's native people who have not benefited from a rich profit-making resource so near their homes.

Our continuing use of SUVs, Humvies and other inefficient vehicles is an example of wastage for which our children will pay dearly some day. Our wasteful ways are hastening the depletion of our fossil fuel resources. We have put ourselves into an increasingly untenable situation by becoming very dependant on oil to maintain our affluence. We pay insufficient attention to developing public transportation or energy alternatives to shift from our petroleum addiction, as we must—the sooner the better!

Despite touting our "democratic traditions" (now being compromised), Western Europe and the United States have dominated the rest of the world by their military and economic power during the last two centuries. Although not acknowledged by the government, for decades "oil security" has been one of two driving forces of United States foreign policy. Witness the U.S.'s hostile involvements since World War II with Iran, Saudi Arabia, Libya, and the Kuwait and Iraq wars. The United States has used up most liquid petroleum within its borders, and for decades our petroleum corporations have searched the world incessantly for more reserves and made contractual agreements with other governments where new reserves are found. (The second driving force of U.S. foreign policy has been domination of Latin America since 1823.)

A December 2005 report of the "Voices for Creative Nonviolence" in Chicago explained "Production Service Agreements" (PSA) for development of oil fields in developing countries. The full report about these agreements, which have been used since the 1960s, can be read online at <www.crudedesigns.org>. Except for the United States, oil reserves in other countries are "owned" by "the state" and are managed by the government, supposedly with revenues from their development to be spent for needed public purposes. When an oil rich developing country's government signs a PSA contract it retains "ownership" of its crude oil resources, but transfers to the major petroleum corporation full control of production and profits for a contracted number of years.

Under a PSA contract a multi-national petrol corporation recoups ALL "profits" until its initial development costs are repaid, at which time a royalty arrangement with the government that "owns" the oil reserves kicks in at so much a barrel. Thus from the beginning the corporation controls all aspects of development, including "risk management" (security), repayment of costs for maintaining production and making necessary improvements through the years. With a PSA arrangement the multi-national petroleum corporation has no risk at all to its investment. It is virtually guaranteed a profit. And it is possible the government that supposedly "owns the oil reserves" might never get a significant return on the development of its own resource to help its people with schools, clinics, roads, and other public improvements.

Coal was the fossil fuel that sparked the Industrial Revolution in England in the late 1700s, and coal remained the dominant "energy slave" for decades in Western Europe and the United States. In earlier years little thought was given to local air pollution or drainage problems because of ignorance and the importance of coal energy in supporting industrial growth. Digging horizontal and sloping shafts into hillsides came first, then deep mining with vertical shafts, elevators and air blowers, and finally, after development of monstrous excavators, strip-mining became profitable. More than the older techniques and even with bonds and restoration required by law, strip-mining leaves entire mined-out landscapes languishing for years as efforts are made to restore some kind of productivity from the surface of the land.

In industrialized countries mining continues in most areas where it has been going on for generations, but far fewer workers are needed now because machines do most of the difficult and dangerous work. Coal reserves in the United States and China are the largest in the world. However, despite regulations in place, air pollution from coal use in the United States is still a significant problem. China's primary "energy slave" source is coal, and air pollution from coal use for homes and industry is a serious problem in China.

A new coal mining technique was introduced in the 1970s in the Appalachian Mountains of Eastern Kentucky and West Virginia. It is called "Mountain Top Removal" or MTR. As reported in the November 2005 issue of Jim Hightower's *The Hightower Lowdown,* and in the March 2006 issue of the *National Geographic*, this technique gets at relatively level beds of coal high in the mountains by first clear-cutting and burning the trees on a mountain top, then removing with explosives and machines the actual top of that mountain to expose a coal layer. The soil and rocks removed are dumped into the valleys below and destroy the vegetation, wildlife and natural drainage system. The exposed layer of coal is then strip-mined away. And when it has been removed, the same process gains access to the next layer of coal.

It is an eerie experience flying over these East Kentucky and West Virginia areas, as I did in July 2006. Scattered odd-shaped mountaintop patches of tan-colored cleared land appear as surprises amid mile on mile of rolling dark green tree-clad mountains. A few MTR areas, probably those that have been mined out, have been planted with grass and appear a very pale green. But most MTR areas are tan colored raw earth, with extensive networks of roads and even huge machines clearly visible from five or six miles in the air.

MTR obviously disrupts and diminishes the lives and property values of those in the valleys around or near the mountain being blown apart and stripped. However, the coal companies that received permission for this process from pliant state governments ignore these facts. Communities have been destroyed by floods caused by disruption of natural drainage systems in mountain valleys and by sudden breaks in earth dams that surround settling ponds on top of the mountains.

The whole process can be called "ecocide" because it completely destroys a natural environment. Despite claims that the cleared and relatively level mountaintops will be "attractive to developers", it has not happened. The operations require relatively few workers. Most people living in these areas are against

MTR, but the coal companies have money and political leverage (like developers who press to acquire and build in flood-prone areas) so state governments
continue to let it happen. Thousands of "valley fills" have been approved and
hundreds of miles of streams have been buried or disrupted.

Until recently the discovery of new oil and gas fields around the world has kept
ahead of the increasing use of oil and gas. But those days are over. Despite the
temporary drop in late 2006, the price of our limited "one-time-use" oil and gas
resources will climb in saw-tooth fashion over the next decades. Chaos is the
likely result around the world because adequate and reasonably priced alternative energy sources probably will not be available when the world, with its much
larger population and energy demand, hits a continuous high price wall.

Poorer people in developing countries also are vulnerable to skyrocketing oil
prices. Many of them, too, have been weaned away from primary use of muscle
power and depend on imported oil for transport, tractors and other machines
for raising crops for export and electricity generation. Having been weaned
away from self-sufficient farming they also now purchase imported basic food
products. With many such developing countries in or near the tropics, those
living and working in larger cities also have become used to electricity-con-
suming air conditioning. Those living in mid-latitudes also have become used
to air-conditioning as a necessity.

Why have well-educated people and governments of developed nations not
taken firm action to face the end of inexpensive fossil fuels that has been on
our horizon since the early 1970s? There are several reasons. [1] For over a century the economies and power of dominating "developed" nations have grown
with cheap oil. Dominating the world and having enough oil available at
acceptable prices (first from their own resources and then from other parts of
the world they dominate) has been the "normal" way of things. Most government leaders, living in the present only and seeking reelection and not wanting
to upset their constituents, ignore the writing on the wall that the cheap "one
time use" of liquid petroleum is coming to an end soon. The profit-oriented
energy corporations, entertainment industry and media, looking only to protect profits now, are not helping the public to understand the gravity of these
realities.

[2] The people in better-off countries also are in denial, unable to come to
grips with the idea that their comfortable way of life depends on the resources
and low wages of people in "developing nations", who now and understandably

are hoping for and even demanding a better way of life for themselves. Furthermore, people in the better off countries seem to think they have an entitlement to these resources. They do not understand that our neighbors in developing countries are as entitled as we are to benefits from the Earth's resources and a better life. Fulfilling their aspirations would require developing and harnessing a vast number of new "energy slaves" and sharing the Earth's wealth.

As for the United States, perhaps there is a third reason [3] why so little has been and is being done to prepare for the time when relatively inexpensive oil and gas will no longer be available to power our nation. And that reason is the power of our corporations over members of our White House, Congress and state capitols.

The lobbying power of United States corporations is among the strongest in Washington, DC, resting in part on an 1886 recording mistake of a Supreme Court decision which has given American corporations the status of persons in the eyes of the law. This recording error was made following a May 1886 Supreme Court case (titled "Santa Clara County vs Southern Pacific Railroad" that had nothing to do with corporate personhood) when a court clerk made a summary "headnote" that included the phrase "corporations are persons". Lawyers jumped on that recording error and have been using it as precedent since that time, reinforcing it with each citation for over a century. For more information on this democracy-busting recording "mistake", refer to a July 3, 2006, Internet item: <http://www.alternet.org/module/printversion/38406> and items listed in the Bibliography and References.

In the last two years there has been wide acknowledgement that oil producing countries are at or past their peak levels of production and that production has reached a "tipping point" beyond which production will continue to draw down ever dwindling reserves until they become too costly for "one-time-use" in our vehicles. In July 2006 a barrel of crude oil was trading (briefly) at over $75. With high prices for oil Canada has become very active in working oil tar resources in its western provinces, a process that uses large amounts of its natural gas and water. To further complicate the energy picture in the years ahead, China's and India's demand for fossil fuel energy is only beginning. Their use of autos and trucks is suddenly on the rise. Already China is firming transactions for long-term oil delivery from Venezuela, Nigeria and other countries that have reserves and production.

President Bush in his 2006 State of the Union address for the first time mentioned the U.S.'s "oil addiction". But he could not have been sincere about that issue because he did not call for any legislative action to reduce our use of gas-guzzler vehicles, to support research efforts at a significant level to develop alternatives, or to tax the excess profits of the oil mega-corporations. In fact, his address looked toward even more dependence on fossil fuels for the next decades. That was no surprise because of the long and deep involvement in the oil business of our President, his family and friends—that include the Saudi family of oil rich Saudi Arabia.

In July 2006 Cuba announced it had discovered and will be developing significant offshore oil reserves beneath waters off Cuba's north shore. Many petrol companies around the world are keenly interested. And, predictably, so that U.S. firms would not be left out of this opportunity to help develop and then import Cuban oil, a U.S. news item said it is likely the Senate will review our decades old stringent sanctions policy against Cuba! It is about time. Obviously our ill-advised sanctions policy has not dislodged Fidel Castro; our policy only disadvantages the Cuban people, and ourselves.

To review, we are in the last throes of the "Petroleum Age", with its deep dependence on a resource we are fast using up. The Near East for decades has had—and still has—the world's greatest petroleum reserves, but even theirs will last only a few more decades with increasing production and use. Almost everything that our vaunted "Western Civilization" represents, in hi-tech communication, factories operated by robots, international air transportation, comforts and conveniences, vacations and more leisure, AND even to a certain extent our "democracy" itself, have been made possible over the last two centuries by the relatively inexpensive energy of fossil fuels. Unless adequate alternatives are phased in and "ready" when we hit the high price wall, all of our vaunted advantages will be in jeopardy.

The United States and China have large coal reserves, but even that, with increased use, would last only several more generations. And with present technologies the use of coal also would exacerbate air pollution and climate change. Like Canada's large reserves of oil tars, the United States has large reserves of oil shale in our western states. But to recover oil from these takes large amounts of energy and water, and oil tar and oil shale resources also are limited resources. In an energy emergency our demand for more energy could encourage "leaders" to abandon environmental concerns in order to develop these fossil fuels. However, such unwise actions would only get us "off the hook" energy-wise for a few decades, and a "day of reckoning" would then be coming through climate change, a shortage of energy, AND a shortage of fresh water!

With higher and higher costs for a dwindling supply of fossil fuels and with no adequate replacement energy sources at hand, what will our children and grandchildren do? The people of the world are between a rock and a hard place in making difficult decisions, but our grandchildren will be in more difficult straits with a reduced quality of their daily lives and enormous tax bills to pay for the misadventures of our generations. And unless we do something, population will continue to soar, further reducing the Earth's ability to support us.

Unless we abolish war by adopting a Limited Global Government, we probably will see desperate governments—even "democratic" governments—promise everything and go to war to secure a few more years supply of oil—and to divert attention from mounting domestic problems and unrest. Of course, the wars, probably preemptive wars again, could be trumped up "against terrorism" and against some poor oil-rich developing country that has invaded no one but has been made an "enemy" by government and the media. In such a war, tanks, military aircraft and humvee-like vehicles will use up enormous amounts of the world's limited supply of petroleum, reducing even more quickly the world's remaining supply.

Oil wars may sound like the story line of a science fiction movie, but it is reality. Were Kuwait and Iraq science fiction? Some world almanacs don't include in the history of Iran the disruption and violence that followed our CIA's 1953 ousting of Iran's elected leader, Mossadegh, after he nationalized Iran's oil fields so his country might gain a better share of the profits. Following Mossadegh's being pushed from power the U.S. reinstalled the Shah and we all remember the 1979 American embassy hostage drama that dominated Jimmy Carter's presidency. Is there any wonder why the United States is no longer viewed in the Near East and throughout the world as a "beacon on the hill" for good?

Would a major conflict involving many nations fighting over oil be Armageddon? Of course not. It would be destruction, killing and chaos brought on because humans did not use their abilities to think and adopt new ways that new circumstances called for. It would reflect adults using childish methods and obsolete religious beliefs in efforts to solve global and national problems. It would reflect adults ignoring their basic religious values and thinking and acting selfishly only for themselves. Difficult times are likely to come during the transition years to alternative energy sources. But much more difficult times will come if humans do not use their intelligence and compassion to deal with the end of the Petroleum Age before it is too late.

Solutions? Is there a way out? I wish I could report very positively that some kind of energy crisis can and will be avoided. I can't. There seem to be encouraging new technologies on the threshold of commercial development that might help, including geothermal, but petroleum prices will continue their rise and there are few signals from government and media leaders to help people deal realistically with the looming energy crisis. (See Appendix C.)

In July 2006 one of the "Car Talk" brothers on radio (Tom and Ray Magliozzi) proposed a $3 per gallon tax on gasoline. His proposal had several purposes. It would discourage manufacture and use of wasteful vehicles. It would discourage frivolous driving. It would provide funds for alternative fuel research and development, and it would support development of public transportation. Such a tax surely would get the attention of the American people and begin to reduce our heavy dependence on fossil fuels.

An Earth Policy news item (Earthpolicynews@earthpolicy.org, Plan B Book Byte 2006-4, April 12, 2006) calls attention to a 2001 Swedish law that shifted tax revenues from incomes for ten years to address environmentally destructive activities which include cars and trucks. Apparently five other European countries also have adopted strong tax reforms that address environmental issues. So there are ideas out there and things are happening.

Is hydroelectric power an answer? Hydroelectric power provides only about 2% or 3% of the world's energy. Most of the world's hydroelectric power potential has been developed and so this source does not offer much additional potential for the future. Furthermore, dams of any size destroy natural systems. Hydroelectric power generation also has its own problem if the watershed behind a dam is mismanaged and erosion takes place. After only a few decades silt is likely to partially fill a reservoir, reducing its water storage capacity for power generation and other uses. Remember my comments about Egypt's Aswan Dam. The heavy spring rains of 2006 in northeastern United States brought attention to the problem of old dams, many of them partly silted up, which no longer produce power, and endanger the people who live downstream.

Is nuclear power the answer? Most of France's electricity is generated from nuclear power plants and several European countries are expanding their nuclear power facilities as they are facing the end of the Petroleum Age. The leaders of Iran also want to develop nuclear power so they can sell their oil, and this is a reasonable long-term government policy.

However, up to now four problems stand in the way of this alternative solving our civilization's imminent energy shortfall. Decades ago it was anticipated that atomic power would provide energy so cheaply that it would not be metered, but that was before its dangers were understood. **One danger** and problem is to provide safe disposal of radioactive waste materials from nuclear power plants, with some waste materials that remain dangerously radioactive for thousands of years. **Another danger**, as in case of equipment failure at Chernobyl in 1986 (then in the Soviet Union, now Ukraine), is the radioactive fallout danger to those living nearby and for miles downwind from a nuclear power plant with equipment failure. **A third danger** is the disposal problem of nuclear power plants themselves as they age, become obsolete, and must be abandoned. As if these problems with nuclear power generation are not enough, there is **a fourth problem** with nuclear power providing the long-term answer to our energy needs. Uranium ore is a limited resource. Estimates vary from a few dozen years to hundreds as to how long supplies will last at current rates of production. But many more reactors are being built and will be built around the world as nations face the demise of cheap oil.

There is always the possibility that new technologies may be invented to solve these problems or that other material might be used for nuclear power generation. But that raises again the fundamental point in planning for the future: We should only plan for the future using technologies that are in hand. To do otherwise is foolish and will only continue the march of all of us—including our children and grandchildren and our civilization—toward and over the cliff, like a herd of lemmings.

Solar and wind power are being adopted more and more, and that is encouraging because they offer pollution-free and virtually unlimited energy. The amount of energy the sun constantly pours into space is staggering and it was mentioned that the Earth intercepts only one six-trillionth of it. Even that micro-fraction is thousands of times greater than the amount of energy used on Earth or is likely to ever be used. Also, humans tap only a small fraction of the potential wind power that is generated by the mechanics of our climate and weather.

Israeli scientists are among the world's most successful in developing and improving technologies for capturing solar energy. Denmark produces most of the wind power machines that are in use, and Germany actually produces more power from wind than any other country. However, developing solar and wind power and all alternative technologies now available will not provide for more than doubling the present demand for energy that is expected throughout the world in the next two decades.

Again I mention Buckminster "Bucky" Fuller, the very original inventor and "out of the box" thinker of last century. Decades ago he proposed a global power grid that would interlink all power generating utilities worldwide and have them operating on a steady 24 hours per day schedule. His idea was that the power generated anywhere would be/could be conveyed everywhere in the world by a global network of interlinked UHV (ultra high voltage) power lines. By Fuller's calculations "power shifting" would provide an abundance of power for the entire human family for generations.

Fuller's proposal for a global grid itself is sound, but also is obsolete because it was based on fossil fuel using utilities. Michael Kessler, a musician and World Government enthusiast, has updated Fuller's proposal. His idea is to build solar power plants in desert and semi-desert areas throughout the world and connect them with a Fuller-type global UHV grid. Most fossil fuel power plants would be phased out. Thus, as the Earth turns on its axis, surplus power would be transferred continuously from solar powered plants in the daylight half of the world to the shadow (twilight and night) half, with stand-by nuclear or fossil fuel power plants ready to provide additional energy as needed.

Biomass, biogas, biofuels and bioenergy are in the news these days. Plant materials used for heat and energy have a long history with humans since fire was "domesticated". The Industrial Revolution sharply increased the use of charcoal for steel making and wood to produce steam to run factory machines and railroad engines. These intensive uses resulted in the clearing of many of Europe's forested areas and brought on laws to preserve those remaining.

As energy use has skyrocketed and concerns for western civilization's "oil addiction" have increased, so has interest in producing energy from "biomass". In the 20th and 21st centuries, biogas, and biofuels, like ethanol, are being made from plant residues, manure, urban sewage waste, landfill gases, garbage, and even grains.

"Biomass" can be any "bio-material" used directly from plants or plant waste, or a residue of plant material like manure, to produce energy. Any kind of bio-mass generates biogas (basically methane) as the bio-material rots with little or no oxygen. The chemistry of bioenergy production is based on the ability of particular microorganisms to digest plant cellulose and other rough fibers that up to now have had little or no commercial value. In the past many farmers with livestock spread manure from their animals on their fields to enrich the soil, a practice less used now to the detriment of our arable land.

"Swamp gas" and "marsh gas" (methane) have long been known as products of decomposition in and around swamps and marshes. Landfills also produce methane as a constant product of the decomposition that takes place. In recent years the methane is captured at some landfills as another energy source. Because methane is a far more dangerous "greenhouse gas" to the ozone layer than carbon dioxide, its capture and use helps control climate change.

As interesting as it is to use plant waste materials and even food crops like corn and soybeans to produce energy, there are problems in addition to the loss of biomass materials for soil enrichment. For instance, it takes about 6 gallons of water and much energy to produce 1 gallon of ethanol. Also, in several United States Midwestern states there is already significant competition among possible users of grains. What should come first: Feeding humans? Feeding animals? Producing energy to drive our autos and machines? Other uses? What about food for people yet to be born? Furthermore, increasing production of corn and other crops for possible use as biofuel material exacerbates problems of soil depletion, chemical runoff and pollution of groundwater sources.

Other energy alternatives. Besides further development of these several alternatives, there are others, such as geothermal energy that has great potential, and there *are* encouraging new technologies that have been tested and need to be tested further for possible large-scale production. Several of these are discussed further in Appendix C. The practical perfection of any of these new technologies, with government encouragement and support, would be far more useful to the stability of the world and happiness of the human family than more intellectual or financial investments in future wars or computerized weaponry.

Some Conclusions about Energy. Even if the United States emerges from the November 2006 and 2008 elections with a more "people oriented" Congress and administration in Washington, the time is so short before we need sufficient alternative energy sources that will help us retain our basic way of life and democratic traditions. Changes will be needed for so many of us whose lives depend on gasoline powered vehicles and other direct or indirect uses of fossil fuels. Too many people are ready to compromise civil liberties as we seek an always elusive "security". Our long term security can best be realized by abandoning our militarized foreign policy, and sharing more with the rest of the world.

The conclusion of this final chapter of Part A, about the Earth's energy offerings, is that fossil fuels, on which we have depended for about a century and a half, are dwindling down and we need alternatives fast! In contrast to fresh water and arable land, there is no shortage of solar and geothermal energy available for human use and new pollution-neutral technologies are available now that will add to our energy production.

However, none of the new technologies offers an immediate prospect of replacing the volume of energy now generated from fossil fuels and none offers the hope of keeping up with the increasing demand for more and more energy that is likely in the years ahead from additions to world population and production. We all must become more efficient in our use of energy and support efforts to add to energy production in responsible ways.

Shifting from our addiction to oil (and our war-making addiction in vain efforts to gain control of more oil) will not be easy. For the sake of our children and those who will follow them, scientists and politicians—with support from the PEOPLE—MUST take action together on this planet, hopefully through a Limited Global Government, to reduce the world's population and help solve our energy crisis.

PART B: WHAT MAKES HUMANS "DIFFERENT"?

In Part A elements of the Earth's natural systems that support humans and other creatures were examined, shortages of arable land and fresh water and "time problems" with the renewability of forests and soil were emphasized, and local problems with air pollution and the unknowns about climate change were highlighted, along with the urgency to balance human needs with the Earth's bounty.

In contrast, Part B considers the human side of the "Earth/People Equation". How are humans different from other living creatures? What aspects of our world cultures might give us the opportunity to do enough in time to resolve problems that have put human "civilization" on an overpopulated and a suicidal course?

Over 90% of the human genetic DNA code also is carried by most other creatures, and there is similarity to plant DNA as well. So what has triggered the enormous difference between our evolution to now and all other living things, past and present? Most living things are "stuck" in an ecological niche, with basic instinctive abilities being passed on from generation to generation. Their numbers and their survival depend on what happens in that ecological niche.

Perhaps the DNA difference between humans and all other living things derived from many positive mutation glitches over millions of years and the cumulative cultural development in the last two hundred thousand years. Humans are no longer tied to an East African ecological niche. The evolution of our brains and culture have made it possible for humans to explore and occupy the whole Earth.

In the Introduction I spoke of "Human Resources" that include mental and physical abilities and the ability to reproduce, but these attributes are shared at some level by all creatures. It is our reasoning and memory abilities and, even more important, our language ability that have made us so different. Using these special attributes has made possible the development of our culture in its great diversity around the world. However, even though we are no longer limited to a particular niche, we still depend on the Earth's bounty for survival.

Once having begun walking upright, using hands with an opposing thumb, and having developed even a limited primitive language, there was no turning back. To survive in difficult environments, human family groups and clans, fragile and vulnerable compared to many other creatures, had to learn to work together and share. Some other creatures do the same.

All creatures to survive must be able to feed and shelter themselves, so human "economic" behavior is not unique. Many of our innovations are elaborations of natural "foraging" in response to our constant needs for food and other necessities. And many of our technological advances are complex improvements to increase our muscle power and our abilities to see, hear, move and remember. It was their language and memory that helped early humans to teach each other things learned before.

As thinking creatures early humans must have pondered questions for which we still have no certain answers. Where did the Earth, sun, moon and stars come from? Where did life come from? Where did humans come from? Why are we here? What happens at death? More contemplative and imaginative individuals, perhaps leaders or storytellers would have made up stories that satisfied the wonderment of others. These stories became myths that, along with the focus on fertility, were handed down and evolved to become the focus of early religions. Each tribe or community fiercely promoted its own goddess and gods, and religion—then as now—provided the cultural glue for growing human communities around the world.

In the judgment of this writer, Education, Religion, the Arts, and Law, in all their institutional manifestations, are the core of all cultures; they are "what make us human". These also are the elements of our culture through which solutions to our problems have always come and must come. Since the beginnings of the human experiment on Earth, the development of these institutions has differentiated us from other living things and propelled our cultural evolution and increase in numbers. These are the subject of this Part B.

Throughout this book I have referred to all that humans have accomplished and all that humans do as an "experiment"? It is an experiment simply because it is an "unfinished story". We still do not know how it will all come out. Will the human species survive? It is up to us. The human species, struggling at first to survive in small groups and living close to nature, has come a long way, especially during the last few millennia, but more particularly in the last few centuries.

However, despite our accomplishments, will the human species become extinct by overpopulating the Earth and/or letting global warming proceed with its ominous consequences? Will our "civilization" be destroyed as we kill ourselves off and further destroy Earth's environment in massive, futile wars? In an increasingly crowded and impoverished world, will our democratic traditions be compromised away, with those who survive struggling to glean a subsistence way of life? With the many critical global issues facing us now, there is no assurance that the human animal or our cultural accomplishments will survive.

Although human-like creatures and humans have been around for hundreds of thousands of years, I still believe the human family is in its "childhood". I say this because of our mindless "adolescent" greed, arrogance, and thoughtless exploitation of each other and our Earth, and our continuing use of violence and war in a vain effort to solve problems. *I say the human race is in its childhood because such behaviors are not the hallmarks of caring adults or a successful long-term relationship between people and other people or between people and the Earth itself.*

Because of the global issues and the vulnerability of our civilization, the portents from recent years are not good. It is up to us, through education, our religious values and cooperation with every one around the world through a Limited Global Government, to face up to our problems. We must learn to work together and share and reduce our numbers soon or face the dismal consequences.

Part B considers Education, Religion and The Arts, and Law in that order.

Chapter 6

EDUCATION

Robert M. Hutchins, who was President and Chancellor of the University of Chicago from 1929 to 1951 and is now deceased, is quoted in a book by William O. Douglas as follows:

> "It seems probable that we are entering a post-industrial age in which the issue is not how to produce or even distribute goods, but how to live human lives, not how to strengthen and enrich the nation state, but how to make the world a decent habitation for mankind." (The Douglas book is *Points of Rebellion,* Vantage, New York, 1969, p. 15.)

The purpose of this chapter is to present a clarion call about the importance of education, not only for our children and young people, but also to help make the world a better place, and, as Robert Hutchins said, to help us "make the world a decent habitation for mankind". How else can we learn about and deal with overpopulation and other converging crises than through teaching and learning and taking appropriate action?

The term "education" is commonly applied to instruction of our children and young people. For those in mid-life it is called "retraining"; and for older folk the term "learning in retirement" has been adopted. All levels of education are essential if we are to overcome the many critical problems that are before us.

In these early paragraphs I share the conclusion of this chapter: I have no magic proposal that might make some part or parts of our educational system more effective. Helping our four children grow up and learn in our public schools, drawing on decades of teaching at different colleges and universities, and recently helping students in local public schools, all I can do is share the reasons for my belief that the right kind of "education" continues to be critical for the survival and success of this great human experiment on Earth.

Some will say that educating the world's billions on the crises we face will take decades and to avert a worldwide calamity for the human family is an impossible task. However, I know that people *can learn quickly if they must about things that strike at their way of life and the future of their children.*

Let me add a few more "concluding paragraphs" about education. In recent decades the basic family unit in the U.S. has been strained and dissembled in many ways. The steady hand of the "mother at home" has been compromised by the fact that in many families, for survival in today's world, both parents must work outside the home. Both parents should work as partners and share as equally as possible in managing a home and raising a family. Sex-driven marriage, easy divorce, latch-key children, multiple remarriages, and large numbers of families led by struggling single parents have eliminated the stability and clarity of long-term family relationships and child rearing.

This instability has diluted the teaching and demonstration of basic values from parents to their children. Hours of learning about violence each day from television and being overwhelmed by highly focused and enticing advertising are part of the "education" we are letting happen to our children. Too many children stumble into adulthood with immature notions of right and wrong, with no concern for other human beings or their communities, and too many only with notions of being rich or famous.

It should *not* be the role or responsibility of public or private schools to teach basic good manners and "deportment" to children. Teaching decent behavior and right from wrong are a part of responsible parenthood. If the present organization of our family structure is not helping our children toward responsible adulthood, the solution must come through family support reforms and parent education, not burdening the public schools that have a different and very important reason for being.

Perspectives about Education. Most animals seem to educate their young one way or another. For animals other than humans most of the critically important early learning about food, survival and limited communication seem to be built into their instinctive heritage. In our evolutionary advance we are no longer led by instinct. However, in the dimming of our instincts, we have gained new brain skills: the power of reasoning, language and writing, which are now assisted by books and computers. But we are not using those special skills to help our survival.

Humans, having the capacity of choice, too often ignore our own experience. We also ignore the accumulated wisdom and experience of others and continue applying ineffective ways of doing things from the past. Einstein once told us that a sign of mental illness is to keep trying to solve a problem in a way that has already proved to be ineffective.

The apparent addiction of adults to continue to try to solve international problems by wasteful and futile wars is a good example. Another is the way in which we Americans tinker and struggle with health care "reforms" and seem unwilling to learn from others about systems that work well in many countries! Still another—and the focus of this book—is the apparent failure of humans to learn about and accept the reality of the Earth's limited offerings and the inevitable conclusion that, if humans are to succeed as a species with a reasonable quality of life for individuals, the human family must be limited in size.

In times past, education that was required for participation in the "professions" (religious, legal and government) was available largely for children of the wealthy and those with power. The masses of other children continued to be taught informally in the home or by apprenticeships in shops. Public education was not generally adopted in the United States until the late 1800s when it was finally accepted that a democracy "of the people, by the people and for the people" could not be successful without an electorate with at least a basic education.

However, to be effective in a democracy education must go well beyond simple literacy. A person who only knows how to read and write but not how to "think" and make good judgments is a prime target for a demagogue. As Robert M. Hutchins informed us:

> "The reiteration of slogans, the distortion of the news, the great storm of propaganda that beats upon the citizen ... mean either that democracy must fall prey to the loudest and most persistent propagandists, or that *the people must save themselves by strengthening their minds so that they can appraise the issues for themselves.*" (Internet, my italics)

In an off-hand kind of joke, Hutchins also said "We can put television in its proper light by supposing that Gutenberg's great invention had been directed at publishing comic books"! Television, computers and "iPods" *are* great potential tools for serious teaching and learning. However I say "potential" because for most people they are a distraction from important matters and are used mostly for business purposes, casual contacts and entertainment. From the point of view of the owners of the media, television's primary purpose is to present advertising for consumer persuasion and subtle control.

Those in the media and movie producers say they are just "giving the public what it wants". However, except for a few stations, networks and programs, like PBS and NPR, and some documentary films, TV programming and the movies have drifted to the lowest common denominator of "entertainment", emphasizing sports, violence and sex, with skewed and opinionated "news". The commercial media industry, focused only on profits, has sadly neglected a commitment to inform (and teach) the public honestly about critical issues that impact their lives now or in the future. The power of television and the Internet must be far better used if we are to educate the young and adults to deal with the converging crises.

However, can we expect media leaders to initiate such changes that might lead to "the people" (their customers!) meddling with the manipulative and lucrative power the media institutions hold over them? Hardly. And also it is not likely that "government" will come to the rescue of the public's "need to know". The increasing secretiveness of the Bush administration continues to undercut the public's "right to know", and too few people are paying attention.

If "the People" truly aspire to have and maintain a healthy "democracy", parents and the public should press for less violence, sports and sex in the media and movies and more education. It is up to the people!

One hundred and fifty years ago in this country, a free eighth grade education was a controversial idea. And after that, the idea of a free high school education was controversial. It is time to establish public supported college education for every citizen who qualifies for that level of education.

The GI Bill following World War II was one of the best investments the United States government ever made. It helped millions of veterans attend college, and led to a more educated electorate with higher earning power. An enlarged and strengthened middle class pressed for legislation that brought on Social Security, Medicare and workers rights. The higher taxes paid by more educated veteran-citizens throughout their working years repaid "the government" (ourselves) many times over for the cost of this program.

Investments in education (and health care) pay off great dividends for a nation in the medium and long term. What can more effectively serve the long-term stability, security, and productivity of a nation than having a well educated, informed and healthy population? Such a population no doubt would find that its "pursuit of happiness" also was facilitated!

Educating for the Future? As William O. Douglas (Associate Justice of the Supreme Court) said in the book mentioned earlier (*Points of Rebellion*, p. 14), "... much of modern education fills young, tender minds with information that is utterly irrelevant to modern problems of the nation or to the critical conditions of the world." And what *could* be relevant is too often skewed to aggrandize the government and does not tell the "whole truth".

Children are our "walking future". Children are "the citizens and the public of tomorrow". If children and young people are not educated to gain necessary basic information and the ability to think for themselves before they must "take over" as adults, they and their culture (our culture!) will wither. They must learn to pay attention to what their elected officials are doing or not doing. They must learn to sift evidence, adopt attitudes that will support the well being of their families and their communities, and work to solve the serious problems that threaten the Earth and the entire human family. They must learn that the long term "general welfare" of all citizens, not the profits of special interests, must be the focus of governments, and that all solutions must consider the rest of the world.

The public that supports all school systems directly or indirectly was schooled in earlier decades and is sharply divided. Some do not acknowledge that certain issues even exist, while others strongly favor different solutions. Honest knowledge about controversial issues is necessary if young people are to deal effectively with these issues when—in only a few years—they will be in charge of the world. The challenge to present controversial issues fairly rests with fair-minded teachers, administrators, and again the public.

Critical issues like overpopulation are controversial, and they remain controversial until they become so overwhelming that their urgency demands attention and cannot be denied. Then the controversy shifts to solutions. Unfortunately, by that time those favoring different solutions are dug in and efforts to resolve the issues will be many times more expensive to apply. The costly distraction of militarization and the ineffectiveness of war to resolve problems is an issue that is ignored. Global warming is another such issue. Still another costly distraction is the demand to include the teaching of "creationism" in our schools when established scientific evidence clearly supports the age of the universe and the evolution of all life on Earth.

In his book, *The Squeeze: Cities Without Space*(1960), Edward Higbee adds another aspect to our education dilemma. He said, "The average school can cope with illiteracy but it is neither staffed nor designed to develop able and imaginative minds, yet these are truly the hope of mankind." Many schools now have Advanced Reading (AR) programs at several levels, and there are special programs, like Encore in many cities that encourage better students to explore new horizons of learning. In China there are "Children's Palaces" where better students may learn beyond the usual curriculum. We must acknowledge—even in a democracy—that all people are not endowed with the same brainpower or an interest in or enthusiasm for learning.

Therefore, a "one-size-fits-all" and "not-to-offend-anyone" kind of education, which teaches mainly to pass official government tests (As prescribed—without funding—by President Bush's "No Child Left Behind" law), is a shortsighted policy that leads to boring the better students and "dumbing down" the whole process. Along with the heavy emphasis on entertainment and "winning a lottery" in our lifestyle, this approach to public education is rendering the United States unable to compete with others in the new global market or even to survive as a democracy.

In the last couple of decades changes in the global work place have caused business downsizing and widespread unemployment of the young and older, and these dislocations have increased the need for education throughout one's life. Dominated by very profit-oriented multi-national corporations, "globalization" is moving ahead rapidly whether we like it or not, even as all people and nations are becoming more interdependent.

Downsizing and unemployment are part of globalization. No longer do people join the work force of a particular business and expect to stay on and move up until retirement years. Furthermore, too many businesses are changing their support of workers by eliminating health care and even pensions. To stay employable workers need educational "retreads" through their working years.

They also need to develop skills and interests that will enrich their retirement years so they will not become "couch potatoes".

Corporate advertising, the media, and even our schools, have not helped us understand that the wealth and comfort of our "Western" way of life has been and is dependant on the low wages and deprivation of most of the world's people. And yet, that is the basis of much unrest in today's world and the taproot of terrorism. These ideas have to become part of what our young and older people understand!

Howard Zinn's *A People's History of the United States, 1492 to Present* (Harper Perennial, revised 1995), James W. Loewen's *Lies My Teacher Told Me* (Touchstone 1996), and Barbara W. Tuchman's review of war, *The March of Folly: from Troy to Vietnam* (Alfred Knopf, New York, 1984), all argue convincingly that the information taught to young students and the public about important events—including "race riots" and wars such as the Iraq war—is not always accurate or complete.

An item in the *Cincinnati Post*, September 22, 2006, by Dan Hurley states this point very clearly. He notes that high school seniors know little about American or world history.

> "They have no idea what document begins, 'When in the course of human events …' They cannot identify the decade the Civil War was fought, have no sense of the impact of the Great Depression or the significance of the Brown vs. Board of Education case. The Hammurabi code of law, the European Renaissance, or the 20th century struggle [with] fascism and communism are widely unknown to most students…. The most important task of a history teacher is to help students to learn to look at life through the eyes of others…. For mainstream Americans, the 'other' may be minority, racial or ethnic groups, women, immigrants, non-Christians, or people living elsewhere." History textbooks "are almost always written in a single omniscient voice, expressing perspective of the dominant group in society."

A positive "spin" is put on every government action, and whistleblowers are not treated kindly. Misinformation is presented to gain support for wars that otherwise might not be accepted by the general public. Lies are invented and spread to generate hate for an "enemy". That kind of behavior by kings, rajahs, emperors and the like in the past can be understood as a reflection of things as they were "back then".

However, I can not accept those actions by leaders in a democracy—who gain their power directly from the people and supposedly are servants of the people and accountable to them. Our presidents and leaders must not indulge in lies and deception while fostering policies based on fear, policies that erode civil rights, and policies that favor particular businesses. Yet it happens.

For nearly two centuries the primary focus of U.S. foreign policy has been to further the business interests of American corporations around the world, with repeated support by the U.S. military. As Robert Koehler said in an editorial (bkoehler@tribune.com), reprinted in the *Carbondale Times*, September 13-19, 2006,

> "Most U.S. military and quasi-military operations of the past century plus have.... served the interests not of the public but of various multi-national corporations.... under the banner of.... Manifest Destiny, anti-communism, war on terror, far from protecting your freedom or mine.... They have promoted global poverty and instability and generated an undercurrent of intense anti-Americanism."

Koehler goes on to quote Marine Corps Major General Smedley Butler, who said, after he retired,

> "I spent most of my time being a high class muscleman for Big Business, for Wall Street and for the Bankers.... I helped in the raping of half a dozen Central American Republics for the benefit of Wall Street."

Everyone should read the books mentioned to learn important things about history we were NOT taught in school, but which everyone should know to understand today's world and to deal with today's challenges. The next paragraphs share items that are not taught in our schools and which our media has not made clear to the voting public.

In recent years we have learned how our nation's very positive long-term legacy has been badly tarnished among the people and nations of the world by our preemptive Iraq war, our blind support of Israel, and our endless and apparently ineffective "war on terrorism" that has run on longer than World War II. During the fall months of 2006 it strongly appears that our "leaders" in Washington are trying to prepare the United States public for a preemptive attack and war on Iran. With our President's record of dishonesty with the American people, should we automatically disbelieve what Iran's leaders say about their intended peaceful use of nuclear power simply because our President and his administration say the Iranians are lying?

The sudden open war between Israel and Lebanon (July 2006) again reveals how unbalanced news has for decades given American citizens a skewed picture of the Near East. United States support of Israel's massive retaliation to Hezbollah attacks (which followed Hezbollah capture of two Israeli soldiers) delayed a cease-fire for weeks, thereby causing hundreds more deaths and much destruction. News reports were quick to say the Hezbollah were receiving military materiel from Syria, but of course did not mention that the United States has always been the source of most of Israel's massive military might, including the cluster bombs that were ("illegally"!) used on Lebanon's civilians.

Israel says it started the war to gain the release of those two captured Israeli soldiers. However, we must not forget that Hezbollah was organized in the early 1980s to fight Israel's brutal occupation of southern Lebanon that has lasted for decades. Further, Hezbollah immediately offered to release the two Israeli soldiers whom they had captured in exchange for many Lebanese citizens and Hezbollah soldiers Israel has held in prison for years. Israel refused and began the open war.

The Arab-Israel conflict has been going on for at least three generations and its resolution must be the keystone to any solution to strife in the Near East. The roots of that conflict go deep, but it has been sustained by the United States' mostly one-sided support of Israel since the U.N. brought Israel into being in 1948. The United States cannot be "for democracy" in the Near East and then not accept an election that was judged to be fair, as happened in Palestine in January 2005 when Hamas won a majority of seats in the Lebanese legislature.

Looking to another region of the world, Latin America, for almost two centuries the United States has consistently and openly opposed any movements by the people toward more democratic government. The United States government has routinely sided with authoritarian governments (despite facades of democracy) and corporate interests. During Reagan's presidency, the U.S.'s secret support of the "contra" in a war to oust the fairly elected Nicaraguan government is an example. The U.S. press always labeled Daniel Ortega and his Sandinista government as "Marxist" although there were fewer "Communists" in the Nicaraguan legislature than in governments of European countries with whom we had normal relations. The problem was that Reagan's government would not tolerate a small country in Central America not accepting domination by the United States and its corporate interests.

Why share these paragraphs of political talk in a chapter on Education? Education to serve the future effectively must be truthful and balanced and we should not assume that essential education happens only in classrooms or in a person's early years. Adults, who should have learned to spot hype, bias and skewing in the news and advertising and should not assume that their governments and corporations are always telling the truth. We the people must have our minds open to learn new things about the world that will affect the long and short term future of ourselves and our families. As we know so well with the unending war in Iraq, with skewed news and lies even democracies can be led into unwise conflicts.

Geography Soapbox Again. In this section on education, I again mount my Geography Soapbox! It is obvious I believe geography has a lot to offer "education to serve the future". The people and even most of the leaders of the United States are woefully ignorant about the Geography of the World, or even "how the world really works" (or does not work well) for most of the human family.

How did we get such an incomplete, skewed view? There are several parts to the answer. The roots of the distorted worldview of most Americans go back many generations. A look at geography books used in the past might help us understand part of the reason our view of the world has been so backward for so long and continues to be myopic. From my collection of old geography texts, an 1831 book, *Geography for Children* by Rev. J. L. Blake published in Boston, draws heavily on religious stories and uses a question-answer "catechism-like" format. For instance, in answer to the question: "What is said of the people of Africa?", the answer presented (that children were to memorize and recite) is "Most of them are remarkable for the blackness of their skins, and for their ignorance and barbarism." And in response to "What is said of the Hottentots?" (in South Africa), the answer is, "They are an ignorant, stupid and filthy people." Could such views have reinforced the support of slavery in the South?

Even after the Civil War and the abolition of slavery, an 1875 book is not much better: *Colton's New Introductory Geography* informs us that in French, British, and Portuguese settlements of Africa the native inhabitants "are Negroes, and are generally in a barbarous condition" and that the inhabitants of Abyssinia "are a handsome people, but rude and brutal in their habits and customs."

There was no foreign reporting to counter such distorted views of the rest of the world. Small wonder that feelings of American superiority followed from such teachings! Small wonder also that Americans and others supported missionaries to go to Africa to "convert the natives" from their "pagan" religions.

Geography textbooks have improved, especially since World War II, as world knowledge increased and communication improved, and through the years many people have taken a geography course at some level in school. However, most teachers have had little or no training in teaching geography or learning from maps. Too much emphasis was on learning the capitols of states, major cities, rivers and mountains, and the important products of countries. Those items are a start, but a start only. They are like trying to learn about the human body by studying only the skin! Global problems and issues were rarely mentioned, and human rights and environmental issues had not yet become a general concern.

In its constant coverage of the tragic wars in Iraq and Afghanistan our media cannot help but give some insight—even only as the incidental background of news photos—into the lives of the people and their homes, clothing, cities, villages and landscapes, perhaps as they are being destroyed. We also get a tragic insight into people's lives when we see the results of tsunamis and earthquakes. But usually in regard to people in other countries, nations and cultures we hear only about riots, wars, assassinations, and the unusual.

Geography as a separate study is no longer taught in grades K-12 in most schools. I know from helping middle school students that some of geography's important subject matter and perspective *is* included in "social science" or "social studies" textbooks now used. That might give hope for a better understanding of the world when our young people grow up. However, the critical proviso in that hope is: *honest information must be supplemented enough for it to be useful in later years,* when, as adults, they "take over the world".

But why is our media so myopic and why does it include very little news from the rest of the world which is so large, so interesting, and on which we depend so much? Admittedly ours is a large country and much is going on. Throughout our entire history we have focused on ourselves. We have been taught about our nation's riches in natural resources, our dramatic spread during the 1800s to the West coast that included overcoming "hostile Indians"— whose lands we were fraudulently taking away. And implicit in our teaching is how clever we have been with our inventions to become so well off and comfortable in comparison to most others on the planet. We have been schooled that what we believe and how we do things is the best. Further, what goes on in the rest of the world is so far away that, in the view of most Americans, it does not seem to impact our daily lives (especially when we are not told!). We ignore it except during natural calamities and war times when "our boys" (and girls!) are at risk. It has been that way for a long time.

So our media carries only limited coverage of 95% of the world's people and ignores global issues that will upend our way of life if not addressed! News coverage in the U.S. starts almost every day with what the President says or does, but we hear too rarely about positive accomplishments of the U.N. in dealing with problems around the world. We hear little about programs or ideas developed in other places that might help resolve problems here at home? Can we do well in the future being so uninformed and uncaring about the rest of the world and about critical issues? We cannot.

Americans can learn much from others. For instance, we could learn much from European countries' adoption of "green" measures to maintain their environment. With the world having passed "Peak Oil", we all could learn from the manner in which Cuba has maintained a reasonable way of life for most of its people since its oil imports plummeted after the break-up of the Soviet Union in 1991. We could learn from many countries how they provide excellent health care to their people at much less cost than our non-system, which caters to the insurance industry. A solid grounding in teaching and learning about the rest of the world is essential.

Teaching of Values? Should our public schooling include the teaching of values? As noted at the beginning of this chapter, the primary responsibility for teaching values should rest with the family and also our religions. Children and young people (should) spend more time at home than they do in school and the responsibility for teaching values and morals goes with parenthood. Parents should be living examples of the values they want their children to emulate. Good classroom management will help reinforce good values in fairness and getting along with others, but the primary responsibility rests with parents at home, reinforced also by the family's religion.

Should public schools teach about religion and permit prayers? In geography and social studies classes when a particular country is being studied it is appropriate and necessary to teach some basics about religions and religious beliefs that are important to those people. These could include the religion's view of the world and its openness to changes that might help the people. In this kind of application, information about religion should not be judgmental or critically comparative, whether it is about Christianity (or any of its hundreds of denominations), Judaism, Islam, Hinduism, Buddhism, or any other religion.

As for having scheduled times for prayer in school or at special school events, I believe whether or how one prays is a very personal matter (Matthew 6:5-7). Individual students can pray by themselves when and as they wish, without group prayer and without intervention by the teacher or school board. In the next chapter I have more to say about the power of religion and I present a challenge to all religious people.

Conclusion. I have touched on many aspects of the educational process. And it should be very clear that I believe education for children, young people and adults is a key to solving the problems that are coming at us from all directions. And those problems include the critical overpopulation focus of this book.

Using our reasoning, memory and culture-building powers, humans have made wondrous advances largely through our communication and educational skills and innovations. However, we still are in our childhood in how we deal with each other. We must develop ways that will make possible the success of the entire human family on this planet.

Educating our children and young people is one of the most honorable, difficult, important, and least rewarded tasks anyone can take on in any country, and it is of critical importance for the survival of the human species and democracy. In totalitarian countries the curriculum is more likely to be dominated by rote learning of basics and blind obedience to and glorification of the government and its history.

Democracies should make sure they do not fall into that totalitarian trap. A democracy depends on "an informed electorate" made up of citizens with the knowledge and will to make intelligent choices at the polls. As we know from the U.S.'s 2000 and 2004 elections, as well as elections in Ukraine and Mexico, democracy depends not only on voting but also on each citizen having confidence that his or her vote will be counted honestly!

Honest education about how the world works, about the converging crises, about the importance of the "People/Earth Equation" and the "People/People Equation", about the need for a Limited Global Government, about the U.N.'s programs, limitations and needed reforms, about logic, propaganda and conflict resolution.... all of these should be included in some way at all levels of instruction with more advanced information being presented at higher levels of instruction from grade school through university.

These are essential if our children and young people are to become the enlightened citizens and leaders we want them to be. How they will lead and how they will vote when the world is theirs depends in large measure on what they learn at home and at school now.

CHAPTER 7

RELIGION (and THE ARTS)

In a May 2006 interview with Alice Chason, Madeleine Albright said it is up to world leaders and diplomats to seek a greater understanding of how the power of religion can help solve global conflicts. I would say it should be up to individuals—as well as the leaders—to humbly apply the power of their deepest values to help solve global conflicts. Albright also noted that common ground must be found among the "three great Abrahamic religions" (Judaism, Christianity and Islam). I couldn't agree more.

The purpose of this chapter is to consider how "religion", and especially how members of the three great Abrahamic religions, might become a more powerful force in helping the human family resolve the converging global crises, including overpopulation. I know that abortion as it relates to overpopulation is a hot button religious issue that involves several ethical considerations. I will address these in the chapter on Overpopulation.

My hope is that this chapter will help religious people focus on the basic values of all religions and not on beliefs or theological details that through the centuries have split religions and denominations and have brought thousands of new "denominations" and "religions" into being.

Many species have come and gone in the Earth's long history; many others have become extinct at the hands of humans. Given the Earth's history, the coming and going of many species, and how I believe the universe works, whether the human species survives does not appear to be of great consequence to the Earth, the universe, or even to "God", "Jehovah" or "Allah".

That may sound grim and contrary to beliefs about a loving God who knows our every action and who surely would not let the human family become extinct. The above paragraph is not meant to be distressing. It is meant to help us to understand the realities of our time and then to do something about those understandings.

In a TV interview on August 20, 2006, Karen Armstrong, a prominent author of religious books, shared the following profound thoughts. Each one is worth pondering: Religion is not about beliefs.… Religion is a form of ethical alchemy.… At its center religion's goal is to engender human compassion.… The originators of all religions had forgiveness and peace at the core of their message.… We should not presume to enlist God (or Allah) to justify our human ethical failings. I do not remember Armstrong using the words "heaven", "hell", "being saved" or "Jesus" in that interview.

I like her inclusion of the words "ethical alchemy" and "compassion". In her writings she also said, "stridently parochial certainty (about religion) could be lethal" and "the one and only test of a valid religious idea … was that it must lead to practical compassion" (Internet).

Besides working, producing and consuming, our lives must have other very important dimensions, like love, compassion, curiosity, wonder and awe, all of which surely are religious impulses. It also is (or should be!) an ethical and a religion-based desire NOT to leave our children and grandchildren (and those who will follow) with problems that will make their lives more difficult.

In this book's Introduction I noted that "attitudes and beliefs", elements of "Human Resources", are important in influencing how people living in a particular area perceive the potential of the environment around them, how they deal with "strangers", how they see the future, and how they deal with change. Attitudes, beliefs and belief systems are the stuff of religion and exert a strong influence on the development or stagnation of a culture. Some cultures and religions are deeply rooted in the past and discourage change. Other cultures and religions are more open to new thinking, problem solving, innovation and change, hopefully to improve the lives of their members and all people. Cultures change through time and so do religions.

Regardless of one's nominal religion (if any), one's "true religion" is the set of beliefs and values that direct how an individual actually conducts his or her life each day. The religion of most people probably carries on from the religion and family values learned during childhood. Others may change their religion based on study, experience and reflection. Further, and entirely apart from any religious institution, one's "true religion" might be a driving desire to become wealthy or to have power over others. One's operative "religion" also could develop from feelings of oppression, revenge or hatred, as must be the case for many involved in tragic Near East conflicts.

There are dozens of religious beliefs and scientific theories, but no one knows with certainty why we are here or how and from what the universe was formed. To bow in faith to ancient myths other humans have invented in their search for answers is not an adult way to answer questions or solve problems. I am reminded of what Mark Vonnegut said to his father, Kurt Vonnegut, who had asked him "Why are we here?" Mark's direct answer was: "We are here to help each other through this thing, whatever it is." That might seem like a sarcastic or simplistic answer, but even the phrase "whatever it is" has deep religious meaning because, in all honesty, we do not know. "Life" is a mystery. The challenge for the human family is to make the best of it—together—in the here and now with what we do know about ourselves and our Earth home, and then let the issue of "heaven", if there is one, take care of itself.

A number of "Dead Sea Scrolls" were discovered in 1945 in caves by the Dead Sea, and since then other ancient manuscripts have been found in the Dead Sea area and also at Nag Hammadi in "Upper (southern) Egypt", in Ethiopia and elsewhere. Through the decades these writings have been translated and presented in many books. Other books have interpreted these documents and raised questions that relate to the beginnings of Judaism, Christianity and Islam. The questions raised are significant in these days when many members of the three Abrahamic religions hold beliefs that derive from these ancient documents and preliterate traditions.

Within each of the "Holy Books" of the Abrahamic religions there are numerous contradictions and inconsistencies. The five books of Judaism's Pentateuch were passed down orally by storytellers for millennia and finally written down thousands of years ago by scribes. And, humans being humans, modifications surely were made in the telling as well as mistakes in the transcribing. An interesting book about similar transcription modifications as they relate to the New Testament is Bart C. Ehrman's *Misquoting Jesus*, published in 2005 by Harper/San Francisco. The research and writings of biblical scholars deepen our insight into how human decisions brought both Old and New Testaments of the Bible to include what they include as well as to gain some understanding as to why some writings were left out. Islam's Koran also has its share of inconsistencies. (Internet: "Bible Inconsistencies" and "Koran Inconsistencies".)

In this writer's view, the Holy Books of all religions are to be revered not as God's inerrant word, but as the rich history and heritage of tribal and other groups in the Near East and India who were among the earliest humans to establish and write down rules for getting along with each other and how to worship their god or gods. With that perspective these writings help us understand our heritage as well as who we are as a human family on Earth in relation to the great unknowns about the universe and ourselves. With that perspective we can learn from all Holy Books and use their wisdom to help us toward a better day in our time.

To survive, the human family cannot afford a continuation of divisive beliefs based on selected quotations from Holy Books. We must not stress verses that pit culture against culture or people against people and lead to war. Beliefs about "chosen people" and beliefs of particular religions or denominations that theirs is the *only* way to God, to "salvation" or a good life, must be set aside or muted. Beliefs about women being formed from man's rib, or the "original sin" concept, that distorts actions that are normal and necessary in nature and among humans, should be set aside. Despicable religion-related events like the Crusades, the Inquisition, the Salem witch trials, pogroms, jihads and the Holocaust, must not happen again.

Religion and Government. From the experience of European countries, the Founding Fathers of the United States established the "separation of church and state" concept as a central tenet of the new government they originated. However, we should not presume that by such a "separation of church and state" organized religion has a monopoly on values, morals, justice and fairness in our daily lives and our governments. Concerns for justice, fairness and "values" should be at the heart of how each of us conducts ourselves each day. And justice, fairness and values also should be on the minds of elected servants of the people in Washington, in our state houses, and in capitols around the world.

Hopefully, in democracies, those who have demonstrated personal and community-supporting maturity and values in their lives are the ones elected to positions of power. Simply being a member of a religion or regular attendance at a synagogue, mosque or church does not guarantee that, if elected, an individual's actions will be legal or in the public's interest or for the "general welfare". Simply talking publicly about one's religion or one's beliefs, as some "leaders" and candidates do these days, demeans their religion but does little for those who are "the least among us and down-trodden".

Are churchgoers more religious or law abiding than others? In contrast to the United States, church attendance is at a minimum in Europe, although crime rates in Europe are substantially lower than in our country. Thus there is no correlation between being a "religious person" and living a crime-free life. Some of those with the most intense (but distorted) religious beliefs seem to be the ones who bomb and kill at abortion clinics, beat up gay individuals, and start wars. They also include those who, having survived the Holocaust, sub-due and occupy another country for decades while they ignore U.N. resolu-tions about establishing settlements in occupied territory. Those with intense religious (or nationalistic or ethnic) beliefs also include suicide bombers in the Near East, as well as those who have trigger fingers always ready on some kind of gun for "retaliation".

Inasmuch as each individual needs shelter and about as much food as other individuals, is it ethically justifiable or fair that some individuals have incomes many hundreds of times greater than most others, while millions are left desti-tute? Are religious people concerned about Jesus' messages about justice and helping the poor? And relating to overpopulation, do major religions—and their members—take seriously the manner in which humans are multiplying rapidly and depleting the planet on which we and our progeny must depend forever for survival?

Are "religious" people really concerned about war and violence—some of it in the name of religion—that dominate the lives of so many on this planet? Do major religions or most of their members pay serious attention to the negative consequences of our culture's deep-seated consumerism? Can the "growth is always better" concept that drives our communities, businesses, profits and population lead to a reasonable future for all?

If our religions are *not* concerned with such questions, we might wonder whether Karl Marx was right when he wrote that religion is an "opiate of the people". The questions cited above are important religious questions that involve the morality and justice in our dealings with others on this planet and our stewardship of the Earth itself. These are the kinds of questions that mem-bers of all religions should be asking each other. These are questions that can help people draw back from extreme individualism and "me firstism" and appreciate how we all are interdependent and must work together if the human family is to be successful in its "experiment" on Earth.

The Challenge of Religious Dialogue. During his long and productive life as a religious philosopher, Henry Nelson Wieman wrote several books, including *Religious Inquiry, Some Explorations*, published in 1969. In the first chapter of that book (page 3) he wrote about the difficulties of discussion among those with different religious beliefs.

> ".... the problem engaging religious inquiry can be discussed profitably only if there is agreement on what the problem is. When there is no agreement on the issues to be discussed, the interchange dissolves into confusion and controversy.
>
> "Religious discussion in great part has been of this sort because the participants are not concerned with the same questions. Some are concerned with what transcends all of time and space; others [are concerned] with a cosmic process that pervades all of time and space; still others with human ideals; still others with interpretation of the Bible; still others with the nature of human existence.
>
> "The basic religious problem is commonly interpreted in such a way as to make these areas exclusive to one another ..."

Can religious people and religious leaders set aside their narrowing and constricting theological beliefs enough so we might work together on important issues of common community and global concern? Can we agree that those who started every new religion probably did so sincerely with a message that was meant to help others?

Can we acknowledge the right of those with religions very different from ours (including individuals with no religion!) to believe as they do so we can work together on issues of common concern? Are there attitudes or understandings everyone might accept that will assist such joint action? It is encouraging that religious leaders of the world already have shown that this can be done and is still being done!

The first "World Parliament of Religions" was held in 1893 as part of the World Columbian Exposition where Chicago's Jackson Park is located today. My comments were too brief in *Healing the World* about that first "Parliament" so I augment them here. Ten of the world's religions participated (Buddhism, Christianity, Confucianism, Hinduism, Islam, Jainism, Judaism, Parsis,

Shintoism and Taoism), and papers on each were presented over 17 days by world leaders.

About three-fourths of the 194 papers presented were about Christianity and were presented with the presumption of Christianity's "superiority" as the "one true religion". As visitors, those representing Eastern religions were gracious not to contest this presumption, although there was a spirited "debate" in the closing session (attended by 7000) between Hindu Swami Vivekanandra from India and John Henry Barrows, one of the Parliament's (American) organizers.

The 1893 Parliament did not result in a generally agreed on final distilling document of consequence. However everything that was said and done was published in 1893 in a two-volume set of 1600 pages that was edited by John Henry Barrows. Furthermore, this first 1893 Parliament was successful in several ways. 1. It was acknowledged as the first meeting ever held between leaders of both "Eastern and Western" religions. 2. It resulted in follow-up dialogues between and among religious leaders who had met at the Parliament. 3. It stimulated the university study of comparative religions in the United States. 4. It encouraged missionaries to be more understanding of native religions. 5. It increased the acceptance of the plurality of religions, especially in the United States. And 6., three-fourths of a century later, the 1893 Parliament led to meetings of world religious leaders that were held in 1970 and since.

Four religious leaders in the United States (Roman Catholic, Jewish, Unitarian and Methodist) held planning meetings during the 1960s which resulted in a large conference that was held in Kyoto in 1970. The conference was attended by over a thousand religious leaders. The Kyoto meeting led to the organization of the "World Conference of Religions for Peace" (WCRP) whose relevant and laudable goal was and is to "forge constructive roles for religious communities in resolving conflict, building peace and advancing sustainable development".

At the close of the 1970 WCRP conference those attending agreed on "Seven Common Religious Beliefs" of all of their religions (Appendix D1). The WCRP has had regular meetings through the years. The seventh assembly, in Amman, Jordan, in 1999, included both Shia and Sunni Muslims, and it has been active in helping overcome the AIDS tragedy in Africa. The organization held its eighth conference in Kyoto, Japan, in August 2006.

There also have been several subsequent "World Parliament of Religions" meetings. "Parliaments" were held in Chicago in 1993; Cape Town, South Africa, in 1999; and another in Barcelona, Spain, in 2004. Parliaments also are planned for 2007 and 2009. Chicago's 100th Anniversary Conference in 1993 developed a seven-point "Declaration of a Global Ethic" (Appendix D2).

At the 1999 and 2004 "Parliaments" the following critical issues facing the world's people were discussed: Environmental stewardship, global sustainability, fair economic practices, religious violence, access to safe water, fate of refugees, and elimination of developing countries' debts. *What can be more important to harness the power of the world's religions than for religious leaders and religious lay leaders to set aside splintering theological differences and apply the core beliefs of all religions to resolve pressing global humanitarian issues?*

In 2005 a group of physical and social scientists published *2005 State of the Future* and included a list of six "Ethical Points for the Future" (Appendix D3). It is instructive to compare the 2005 ethical points with those in the 1993 "Declaration of a Global Ethic". *What better way to give direction and political will to governmental leaders in all countries than to insist on their following a "Declaration of a Global Ethic" and "Ethical Points for the Future"?*

I include the above details about these meetings of thousands of religious and lay leaders because they signal a growing interest among religious and lay leaders in understanding each other's religions. And just as significant as their meetings, is the nature and range of topics of their discussions. Religious leaders of the world, therefore, already have shown they can set aside their differences and focus on the common denominators of their religions and global issues that even now compromise the lives of millions and demand solution.

But can religious leaders bring their parishioners along? It is acknowledged that in their seminary education ministers of many denominations raise and discuss serious questions and learn things about the history of religions they are reluctant to share with their parishioners. So, as complimentary and optimistic as I am about these WCRP and the several World Parliament of Religions meetings, there is a question. The meetings and pronouncements are impressive. But how do these great ideas, distilled by religious leaders the world over, translate into understandings and actions by the millions of members of the many religions that participated in and supported those efforts?

Have the millions of ordinary people who identify with these great religions heard much if anything about these meetings? Do their leaders still emphasize the narrowing views that separate one religion from another? Do leaders of these religions still cling to animosities engendered by ancient events or myths? Can overcoming differences happen between and among some members of the Abrahamic religions whose intolerance and even hatred for members of the others religions has been brought to fever pitch by various world events? The smoldering coals of schisms still feed the flames of inter-religious conflict in the Near East and too many places.

Religious leaders must help their parishioners become more open to working with others of different faiths. They must emphasize the common beliefs of all religions and be less strident in proclaiming that theirs is the only path to salvation and meaningful living. Leaders and members of the monotheistic Abrahamic religions should acknowledge that Jehovah, Allah and God are different names for the same Creator of the Universe they worship. Religious leaders also should be less concerned about increasing the number of their members and more about helping their members become helpful citizens in their communities and the world.

In looking toward resolution of the human family's looming crises, what could be more powerful than the billions of religious people in the world—based on their common beliefs and values—cooperating on the critical "People-People" and "People-Earth" issues? Crucial good work could be done and a renaissance of cooperation could lead to more people actually becoming interested and active in religious work.

Creative Interchange. Considering Wieman's negative 1969 observations on inter-religious discussion which were quoted earlier, the apparent success of the repeated meetings in recent years of thousands of religious and lay leaders seeking common ground in their discussions is remarkable. The number and continuation of these discussions is an indication of the increase in acknowledged religion-related global issues that are crying out for immediate attention.

In a 1946 book titled, *The Source of Human Good* (page 267), Wieman says "Since *creative good* at the level where it saves and transforms human personality always works in the form of *interaction* between persons, we must deal with persons to deal with it." Decades later Wieman's further thinking on this subject brought him to invent the term "Creative Interchange" as the basic concept for unlocking human potential to resolve problems peacefully and lead to a cultural flowering of civilization.

But what is "Creative Interchange" and how could it help? In these next paragraphs I draw from Chapter 5 of David Oughton's unpublished PhD dissertation, *The Implications of Henry Nelson Wieman's Philosophy of Creative Interchange for World Peace* (St. Louis University, 1998). Writing about the importance of "Creative Interchange", Oughton includes this long sentence from Wieman:

> "The human race cannot long survive on this planet with the increase in power and complex interdependence unless the ultimate foundation of community be shifted from culture, race, class, nation, or alliance of nations and from any one of the world's religions and is firmly established on that *creative interchange* which has created the humanity in every individual, from the first days of infancy, no matter (to) what culture, race, class, nation, or traditional religion he or she may belong." (D.E.C. italics)

Wieman believes that each individual survives and becomes human only through this process he calls "Creative Interchange", starting in a family within a single culture. Individuals grow from childhood to responsible adulthood through Creative Interchange with other adults in their own and then other cultures. Wieman's cogent observation is that everything humans have created in their cultural evolution over the millennia has been created through the "person to person" process of Creative Interchange. And finally, Wieman believes all of us, as world citizens striving for world peace and justice, must downplay the divisiveness of race, class, nation and religious differences and acknowledge a higher priority allegiance to and concern for the human family.

Wieman firmly believes we should not seek a "global melting pot" in which everyone will experience a similar "growing up", eat the same foods, learn the same history and share the same values. Instead we should retain and treasure the rich diversity among the world's cultures, a diversity that provides the basis for learning new things from others and thereby provides for a continuing stream of enrichment and creativity. As one suggestion to make a more enriching Creative Interchange possible, all humans could learn Esperanto in addition to their native language. Appendix E has further details about Esperanto as a second language.

Wieman believes that, while we accept the rich tapestry of our differences and our histories, we must adopt Creative Interchange as the ongoing process to resolve issues between individuals, religions and nations. He sees Creative Interchange as the way to abandon war and violence on those with whom we differ. Is this an easy path to take? Not at all, witness Mahatma Gandhi's difficult path in working toward India's independence from Great Britain and the successful but martyred path taken by Martin Luther King in pursuit of civil liberties for blacks in the United States.

Wieman presented three very different scenarios for the human future, and it is not hard to discern in which scenario Wieman believed we were (and are) enmeshed.

1. With no change from the status quo there will be total global war and annihilation.

2. If people become addicted to comfort, pleasure, amusement, sensuality, apathy and consumption and allow a ruling minority to regulate every area of life through brain-washing and propaganda, then an elite bureaucracy will come to dominate the globe and suppress the majority.

3. With Creative Interchange and religious commitment Wieman sees the possibility of a true world community emerging.

I believe Wieman would agree that we are completely enmeshed in scenarios 1 and 2 but that an "elite bureaucracy" has not yet been able to take over the world. However, I think he would agree that the present administration in Washington, D. C. and multi-national corporations are pushing to take over the world for control and profit, and that the "total global war and annihilation" stage is hovering nearby.

Conclusion. "Creative interchange" could *not* teach children "thou shalt not kill" and "turn the other cheek", and years later when they have grown to adulthood tell them, with hyped up "news" about a new enemy, to acquiesce to a government that then tells them "to render unto Caesar, etc...." and "it is now OK and 'patriotic' to kill certain other human beings". Perhaps people with a Scrooge-like mentality might say, "Let wars and disease kill off the surplus population."

It is clear that Wieman's "Creative Interchange" concept, though developed in a philosophical/ religious context, depends on education for its implementation. It also is clear that "Creative Interchange" is related to "Passive Resistance"

(Gandhi's and Martin Luther King's approach) and "Non-Violent Conflict Resolution" (now being taught and used in schools and businesses) as the only adult ways to resolve all conflicts within the spirit and framework of what each of us knows is best. It is the only way that is truly consistent with the basic values of all religions.

Can individuals and church leaders adopt "Creative Interchange" and the other methods mentioned above as adult strategies for solving the critical problems that face all of us and our civilization?

The problems we face have crept up on us so slowly and with too little attention having been given to help us appreciate their linkages, urgency and consequences. We are busy and perhaps overwhelmed with day-to-day needs of our families and our work. We are addicted to the status quo because we are a part of it and that is what we know. We have been brainwashed our entire lives with the belief that wars, just because we have always had them, are inevitable between nations. Incomes, of course, should increase with experience and one's value to a business. We have been brainwashed to accept as normal the many millions of dollars per year incomes of CEOs and the abject poverty that exists among so many. We have been brainwashed that businesses and profits must increase steadily to show "success". We have been brainwashed to believe that the population (membership) of our communities, states, churches—and in some places even families—must also increase to show "success".

Our churches, synagogues, temples and mosques have focused on their particular threads and designs in the tapestry of our different cultures. To help our religions become a more positive force toward a world of freedom and justice, each of us and our religious and political leaders should:

1. Identify the basic values and beliefs that truly underpin our lives and our hopes for our children;

2. Abandon beliefs and values that are narrowing, restrictive or non-fulfilling;

3. Adopt values in our lives that *are* positive and fulfilling, not only for ourselves, but for others with whom we share this planet; and

4. Work with others on the critical global People-People and People-Earth issues to help bring on a world we will be proud to pass on to our children and those who follow.

Unitarian minister Jacob Trapp proposed these thoughts about religion that are similar to those of Karen Armstrong:

"Religion is walking with others, listening to others, sharing with others. It is not a creed but a way of life. To be religious is to be grateful for the much we are given and to give in return as much as we can.... Religion as a set of right beliefs.... becomes divisive and absurd."

Going a bit further with this thought, Dr. Paul Farmer, a young doctor who has devoted his life to help Haiti's poorest, wondered how God could permit the deep poverty that is so pervasive in Haiti. In seeking the answer, and following the "here and now" emphasis of his "liberation theology" point of view, Farmer translated a native proverb as follows: "God gives us humans everything we need to flourish, but he's not the one who's supposed to divvy up the loot. That charge was laid on us." (Tracy Kidder, *Mountains beyond Mountains*, Random House, 2004, p. 79.) The human family must work together to guarantee an acceptable future for all.

Religious people around the world, with their compassion for others and a concern for their children and their grandchildren, must accept the challenge of overpopulation and work together for a sustainable global civilization. It is up to ordinary people like all of us to help our less well off neighbors on this planet to achieve a reasonable level of living, whether they are in Haiti, Zambia or Louisiana. Our REAL religious values—values that come from the heart and look to the future—must be the key to our helping.

*   *   *

"THE ARTS". The "Arts" are closely related to both Education and Religion. "The Arts" also are a part of our being "human" and the several "Arts" distinguish us more sharply than other attributes from all other creatures. We know that pets and primates can be happy or sad, and they play and mimic, but none apparently has developed (on their own) an interest in art forms. I add "on their own" to acknowledge that animals have "learned" to finger paint, to dance, to ride a bicycle, perhaps to count, etc., but they did not learn those skills by or among themselves. And they did not invent finger paint or bicycles!

Since the beginnings of human experience virtually all human feelings and emotions, such as grief, love, elation, awe, sadness, power, happiness and even values, have been richly expressed in various and changing kinds of music, art, poetry, dance, drama and literature. "The Arts" also involves aesthetic senses, the appreciation of form, harmony, color, texture and perfection. All of the arts are essential to our humanity.

These emotions and senses and the many avenues of "the Arts" are manifestations of the spiritual dimension of individual humans and all religions since their beginnings. The arts are not only important for the creativity they engender, they also contribute to mental health and stimulate learning and creativity in other fields. How we manage these emotions and senses also helps us be more effective in learning and doing just about everything humans do.

The future of the human family depends on both "the Arts" and also on physical activities. Every individual needs good nutrition and must have regular exercise to maintain the health of his or her body. We also need good health to permit us to do our jobs more effectively and to participate in "the Arts" and other activities.

I am not a fan of "spectator sports". Being only TV watchers and spectators of games leaves too many individuals with no hobbies and avocations that can touch a spiritual, creative chord and enrich non-working time, especially during retired years. Spectator sports lead too many to be "couch potatoes", to obesity, to artificial adrenaline rushes, to an unsportsman-like "anything to win" mentality by coaches and players, and sometimes to destructive behavior by "fans". Unfortunately such a stress-laden mentality can carry over in attitudes toward all dealings with others, including a nation's foreign policy.

An interest in one or more of the Arts can provide a counterbalance to our highly competitive and stressful "must win" attitudes regarding business, sports and foreign policy. A satisfying interest in and support of the Arts can lead to more cooperative attitudes and use of Wieman's "Creative Interchange". We must support "the Arts" in our schools and communities to help individuals—through active participation—fulfill their spiritual natures, to enrich their lives, and to become better world citizens.

CHAPTER 8

LAW AND "LIMITED GLOBAL GOVERNMENT"

Foraging for food and survival would have been full-time occupations of the earliest humans as they evolved from ape-like forebears. And after hundreds of thousands of years, simple manifestations of education, religion, and the arts would have enriched the saga of humans on Earth. Acceptable rules of behavior also must have come early, but "law" was a later invention.

In my view the advancement of civilization has been based on two things in the political realm. One is the concept of TAXES, in whatever form, hopefully and presumably to be spent wisely for services that those who paid taxes could not provide for themselves, and not for the aggrandizement of their leaders. And the second is the concept of LAWS that have slowly moved toward more complete justice and opportunity for everyone in all communities, large and small. For humans to survive as a species and succeed on this planet, we desperately need to carry law to the next level, global law, the focus of this chapter.

The Beginnings of Law. We know that some living things other than humans live in ordered communities by instinct. Large colonies of bees and ants have definite roles for each individual and maintain a queen; but it is all done by instinct. Wolves and elephants live in groups led by a strong male leader, probably chosen by strength and natural leadership, but the activities of groups of these animals apparently are carried on mostly by instinct.

However, the concept of human rights and the development of codes of laws, especially those that are written down and establish rights for minorities and common citizens, are human inventions that appeared in the human saga only about 4000 years ago. Before then there was no writing and no "law" that pre-scribed—with consistent penalties—how individuals, families and groups of people were to act—or not act—in relation to others.

Human groups must have started with the family and clan, groups of only a few dozen individuals who struggled for survival. All members of such groups would know everyone else throughout his or her life. Rules of behavior between and among individuals and taboos would have been learned early and would have been followed stringently. It seems likely that the most powerful males would have forced their way to be the "leaders". Except for younger and stronger individuals taking over leadership in due course from within or from outside a group, life would have gone on with few changes from generation to generation.

Apparently fertility and goddess-based religious rituals also came early in the human experience, and religion and governing would have been intertwined. Each tribe would have originated its own myths and its own goddesses, gods and rituals, perhaps gaining new ideas and technologies from other groups with whom they came in contact. There were no prisons and decisions regard-ing infringements of rules and taboos would have been handled within the group.

Through time and for greater security several clans would have combined to form a tribe of hundreds or perhaps a thousand or more individuals. The forming of a tribe from several smaller groups meant joining with those who had different gods, goddesses and governing rules, different rituals and taboos. And one could not expect to know all members of the larger community. The dominant group would have forced their rules, taboos and worship of their gods and goddesses on the newcomers. Systems for dealing with complaints would require "courts" and, as groups became still larger, special persons would be "decision-makers" for the larger tribe.

Perhaps the "decider" in such "courts" was the tribe's priestess or priest, its chief, its queen or king. With no written language in the earliest of times, if knowledge of cases and decisions were carried forward at all, it would have been by oral tradition. It was a long time before codes of law finally were writ-ten down in stone or on parchment so that decisions and legal experience could be carried forward more accurately and provide the basis for advance-ment of our civilization and the concept of human rights.

To put the words "chief and king" in better perspective as they are used above, we must realize that many of the "kingdoms" noted in the Bible and later were no larger than a few modest sized counties in the United States, and that the "kings" ruled over only several hundred or several thousands of members, probably from several tribes having been drawn together. Records left by early kings routinely exaggerated their importance and accomplishments. (Are politicians and leaders different now?)

The earliest code of laws of which there is a copy is the Code of Hammurabi, an accumulation of "legal cases" involving property rights, trade, marriage, families, civil disputes, and crimes that had been handed down by oral tradition in the area that is now Iraq. Hammurabi's Code is a record of 282 such cases that were inscribed in stone about 3800 years ago. The upright stone slab was made during the reign of Babylon's King Hammurabi and includes the concepts that the strong should not take advantage of the weak and the "eye for an eye" concept.

Moses' "Ten Commandments", which is a mixture of religion and rules for the Hebrews to get along with others in their community, provides insight into how religion and government were intertwined during these early times. Presented to the Hebrew throng wandering in the Sinai Peninsula in the 13th century BCE, the commandments helped unify the Hebrews in their government and religion as they moved toward Canaan. According to the books of Joshua and Exodus in the Bible, reaching Canaan and following what they believed were directives from their god (as was common of tribal people in those days), they completely destroyed some towns and killed all inhabitants (genocide? ethnic cleansing?) as they advanced and settled the land which their god said was to be theirs. Two of the Bible's books, Deuteronomy and Leviticus, later laid down a detailed set of laws, rules of conduct and extreme penalties by which the Hebrew people were to worship their god and be governed.

As an example of another early "law", the "Cain Adamnan" (or Law of the Innocents) was designed to protect clergy, children and women from violence and capture in wartime. It was agreed to and signed by a large number of Irish leaders and clergy in 697 at Iona near the center of Ireland. (Internet)

Even before the Magna Carta, when the kings of England were struggling to raise money for the Crusades and pay ransom for the release of Richard I from the Holy Roman Emperor, the kings already had made legal promises and concessions to their barons. The Magna Carta was signed under duress by King

John in 1215 at Runnymede, England, when his barons threatened a civil war. The Magna Carta consists of 63 clauses that pertain to all aspects of life, property and business and represented a significant dilution of King John's power. Thus he did not sign the document because of a mature judgment as to what was "right" for his people.

Regardless of the size or nature of the political unit, there always has been concern about the wisdom and honesty of leaders in their dealings with "the people". Because of this many have emphasized the importance of "law" as the basis for our civilization. As Emery Reves said in his 1945 best seller, *The Anatomy of Peace* (Harper & Bros., NYC, page 232),

> "Any political system in which the fate of the people depends upon the wisdom or shortsightedness of leaders is fundamentally wrong.... Our salvation lies not in the wisdom of leaders but in the wisdom of laws."

Laws form the governmental framework by which humans have been able to find more security in larger and larger communities. Over the centuries tribal areas and principalities combined into larger political units, and in the last two or three centuries the combining process has led to the "nation states" we know today. Greater security has opened the doors of opportunity, specialization, and creativity in all fields of endeavor.

Larger political units can provide greater security under law for the common person, even with totalitarian leadership. But, the larger the political unit, the greater the challenge of fairness and justice among the diverse people who will be citizens.

Systems and traditions of law also establish normative procedures for dealing with those outside the country with whom the government and individuals carry on necessary trade and have other relations. We often hear about "international law" that helps regulate matters of contention between and among nations. However, a law system that deals only with and through nations is incomplete.

An effective system of laws must have power to deal directly with individuals who break the law, just as the United States government can apprehend individuals in any state who break federal laws. To fill that gap on a world basis, the International Criminal Court (ICC) was organized and has been operative since 2002 to deal directly with individuals who are accused of participation in genocide, crimes against humanity or war crimes.

Nation States in Our Time. Nation states with systems of laws operating within their borders have served humanity well enough in the last few centuries but only up to World War I. Especially since World War II many things have happened that make the world a very different place from what it was during centuries just past and up to 1914. Regardless of the U.N.'s efforts, for practical purposes, and with each nation "protecting its sovereignty", there is virtual anarchy between and among nations.

For thousands of years with anarchy among groups of people, large and small wars have been the primary means of dealing with serious conflicts. However, regardless of events that may have triggered a conflict, wars do not solve problems and animosities linger on for centuries, many times long after triggering events are forgotten. Serbians still bitterly remember their defeat by the Turks in 1379. During wars in recent centuries both sides tend to abandon concerns about so-called "rules of war" that have been established. When a war finally ends representatives of both sides still must meet around a table. Both victor and vanquished have been weakened but the victorious nation imposes its will on the vanquished, and terms of surrender or "armistice" are likely to plant the seeds of later hostilities. It is acknowledged that the Versailles Treaty at the close of World War I led to World War II. Regardless of the genesis of a conflict, the victors write the history books, justifying all of their actions to win the victory while heaping blame on the vanquished. And through all of this the basic issues that caused the conflict are rarely addressed.

With increasing levels of interdependence among all nations today and the enormous power of air, sea, land and space weapons that are available, war in our time is obsolete as an arm of "foreign policy". An intended or unintended nuclear holocaust could render the Earth virtually uninhabitable for millennia and kill virtually all of the "higher" forms of life.

The vaunted "sovereignty" still claimed by each nation is now a myth that cannot be maintained. Nations, including the U.S., proclaiming their "sovereignty", object to other nations (or individuals from other nations) interfering with their elections. However, the U.S. is probably the world's most persistent meddler in the elections and affairs of other nations since the 1820s in Central and South America and continuing to the present. Consider also that nations and individuals within nations should have the right to make decisions that look toward their future needs, including energy needs. Then consider the duplicity of the present U.S. government in Washington, while controlling the world's largest nuclear arsenal, insisting that Iran may *not* develop nuclear power plants (so they can sell their oil) because the Iranians *might* also intend secretly to develop nuclear weapons.

Many things affecting the function of nation states have taken place since World War II. In my view the ten changes listed below have rendered nation states obsolete in terms of their ability to provide true security and stability for their populations in the 21st century:

1. The colonial empires of former centuries have been dismembered and former colonial people are free to govern themselves, for better or worse. Civil wars and unrest in developing countries have led to a vigorous arms trade, with the U.S. government and industries providing most of the arms sold. (After three years of work, the U.N. General Assembly overwhelmingly passed an Arms Trade Treaty in October 2006, with the U.S. casting the only "No" vote.)

2. The level of economic interdependence among all of the world's people and nations has mushroomed, making every nation deeply dependent on others for necessities. U.S. multi-national corporations dominate this interdependence.

3. The world's population has soared (and is soaring), especially in "developing nations", exacerbating the overpopulation issue and the deterioration of the Earth.

4. The United Nations, another confederation of "sovereign nations", has proved to be no more effective than the League of Nations in stopping wars that involve powerful nations or in eliminating poverty in the world's poorest nations.

5. "International law", slowly developing among nations, has limited value simply because nations cling to their "sovereignty", and the powerful nations do as they please.

6. With no effective global law and with virtual anarchy between and among nations, multinational corporations are steadily gaining in power for the profit of their CEOs and shareholders.

7. "Developed nations" are addicted to using and are rapidly depleting the Earth's fossil fuels, with inadequate actions taking place toward developing replacement energy sources.

8. Global climate change (global warming) is an ominous reality and humanity—through their nation-states—is pressing most of Earth's renewable resources beyond their limits.

9. There is a tragic and widening gap between people and nations in the world who are better off and those who are economically very poor. Even some "developed" nations, including the United States, have a large portion of their citizens living in poverty.

10. And finally, worldwide communication technology has advanced spectacularly and is so widespread that poorer people everywhere are well aware of their disadvantaged situation and are becoming more restive about it.

With deep and increasing interdependence, nation states are obsolete as independent sovereign units. If the U.N. and emerging "international law" are dominated by a few powerful nations, to whom can the world's people turn to resolve global problems that will destroy them and our civilization if left unattended? Perhaps we can gain a larger perspective about *law* from remarks made by Robert M. Hutchins in an address at Simmons College in Boston in November 1960. From the Internet:

> "…. The law is a great teacher…. .The popular notion that law reflects the mores is, as countless historical examples show, often the reverse of the truth. Law helps make the mores (values people live by). Law-making is the process by which the members of the political community learn together what the mores should be."

According to Hutchins, "law" does not have to follow and make order of human actions *after* the fact. "Law" can help make the mores and establish the values people live by! Making and enforcing appropriate new law can lead the public as circumstances demand. That is a lesson the United States Congress and Supreme Court should learn. Not every legal question is answerable from our Constitution that was written over 200 years ago. The many converging crises that face humanity in these early years of the 21st century surely qualify for "leadership by the law".

Yearning for stability and security in their lives, I hope "education" through schools and the media can persuade the masses that some form of global government has a better chance of dealing with the crises than going along with unbridled nation states and their wars as we have in recent centuries.

Limited Global Government. Even acknowledging that the law can be a great teacher, can the diverse people of the world, organizing together or through their governments, deal with divisive issues in an intelligent, caring manner? How can people and their governments come to some agreement on peacefully sharing the Earth's limited resources? Can people be educated quickly to accept the need to reduce the size of families? And how can this be done in countries where large families are important for economic reasons? The way many governments and the media have ignored or played down these problems over recent decades is not encouraging. But our times and the converging issues demand solutions soon. Cooperative action on a global level by the world's people and nations is essential if these issues are to be resolved in time.

The answer, as touched on above, does lie in "something about law". On behalf of the world's people we need to establish law at a level beyond nations. It must be at *the global level* to encompass the whole world. "Limited Global Government" has been mentioned many times in previous pages. It is a concept whose time has come.

Are there new communication technologies or a new approach that might provide a way that makes global government possible now whereas global law and global government were only a dream before? There are both! There are several highly effective new modes of global communication (computer, FAX, cell phone, satellite) and there is a higher level of government called a "Limited Global Government". The words "Limited" and "Global" are the keys.

Most people—even those in developing countries and whether they use the Internet or not—have some idea of the Internet's power to educate and instantaneously inform about what is going on anywhere on Earth. The Internet will prove important in elections from now on, from city hall to Washington to the U.N., and the Internet could become an enabling factor in establishing a global government. We are the first generations to have several globe-encompassing person-to-person and information-sharing communication options available to us.

But what powers would a "Limited Global Government" need that the U.N. does not have, which are essential to its success? Why and how would it be limited? How could any global government address and help solve our converging crises? I will get to these questions.

My first book, *Healing the World*, reviewed the history of world government ideas and efforts, considered the weakness of the U.N., and set forth the reforms needed that could make the U.N. a true Limited Global Government with real powers. It also presented two other ways to achieve a Limited Global Government.

Briefly, the idea of a community of nations is an old one, and many world leaders have favored the concept for generations, including a number of United States presidents and generals. The League of Nations and the U.N. were flawed from their beginnings in the way they were organized. They were (and in the case of the U.N. are) set up as confederations of sovereign nations, like the original agreement among the thirteen American colonies that did not work. In a confederation the central government is not given enough power to fulfill the reason for its being established.

After years of wallowing under the Articles of Confederation, the United States Constitution was written in four months and then over four years (1787-1791) was ratified by the colonies (by some reluctantly) to establish a central government with limited powers. After World War I the League of Nations was established and failed. As for the U.N., immediately after it was formed in 1945, many governmental leaders and others foresaw that it would be seriously hampered by limitations of its confederate structure in fulfilling its goal of eliminating war.

Many agree that "nations" or "nation states" are obsolete and a few pages back I listed 10 reasons that give credence to that point. Critical issues keep getting pushed aside by the media and the governments of many countries. They are being pushed aside in part because to resolve these issues will require significant changes in the status quo of relations among nations and the way many of our businesses and economic institutions function. To do anything meaningful about the critical challenges facing us—including the overpopulation issue—will take more than mere tinkering with the status quo.

Here is a recap of the several critical issues that face us: The world's dwindling supply of liquid petroleum (ignoring the pre-election price drops during fall 2006), deterioration of the Earth's renewable resources, global climate change (global warming), the domination of the world by only a few dozen multinational corporations, military and war expenditures that are leading to national bankruptcy rather than security, and the fact that the world is overpopulated now. In the face of these juggernauts, our way of life is like a house of cards.

It will not be easy to deal with any of these issues. All of them are interrelated in some ways with the others. Elements in their solution will come down more heavily on some businesses and individuals than others. In *Healing the World* I included a section titled "The Elephant in the Room" which explains how some reduction in the United States' Gross Domestic Product (GDP) and personal incomes is likely to happen under a global government's programs to eliminate world poverty. A reduction in the GDP is the "Elephant in the Room" that no one wants to talk about. I go on to explain that such a reduction would actually be good for United States citizens in several ways that I briefly recap here.

So how could a reduction in the GDP and personal incomes be good for U.S. citizens? First we must understand that GDP includes the value of services as well as products. It also includes all costs for the military, war, police, lawyers and courts, prisons, fire damage, auto accidents and all of our medical expenses. By reducing some of these our GDP would decline, but we could have less complicated and happier lives. We should shift most of the money now spent on the military (for which there is no return on that "investment") to support a Limited Global Government and undertake long neglected construction and services that will improve our schools, communities, infrastructure and health services. These shifts would take place over several years during which disarmament also would take place and during which industries could make conversions and become more Earth-friendly.

In the U.S. we should not remain hostage to the insurance industry. By adoption of a government managed universal coverage single payer health care system, we would save money, we would be healthier, we would reduce medical bills and be more productive as individuals and as a community. And the insurance industry would still do well selling their many other insurance offerings as well as supplementary health insurance to those who wanted it and could afford it.

By increasing our non-military foreign aid (through a new global government) and cooperating with the rest of the world we would increase our security, our country would restore the respect that has been squandered in recent years, and we as a nation would feel much better about ourselves. Other wealthier nations also would want to support similar "people programs" in developing countries through the Limited Global Government to alleviate and overcome poverty.

Nations would *not* be dismembered under a Limited Global Government. Nations would continue, just as the thirteen independent colonies have continued as the thirteen original states of the "new" United States of America. The colonies transferred to the new central government certain limited powers; all other powers remained with the states. By granting limited (but necessary) powers to a new global government, nations would continue to function within their borders as they do now.

Powers and Funding of a Limited Global Government. The only direct way to address global issues is the establishment of a Limited Global Government, a level of government above nations. And a new Limited Global Government (LGG) would need the following powers that were not granted to the United Nations in 1945:

1. The LGG would need power to raise money by levying micro-taxes on any kind of international transaction (see below) to support its own operations and functions.

2. The LGG would need funds to support a Global Parliament with definite powers and

3. to support an Executive Branch.

4. The LGG would need to establish and support a Global Peace/Police Force (GPPF) made up of volunteers from around the world to carry on the kinds of "police actions" the U.N. now musters with difficulty. The GPPF would work with the world's nations as they disarm and could assimilate surplus equipment from nations downsizing their military.

These are the kinds of limited powers that a global government *must have* in order to fulfill its mission of eliminating war, poverty—and terrorism.

In addition, as difficult as it would be for "one language Americans", Esperanto should be adopted as a common (neutral) global language for all functions of a Limited Global Government and the Global Peace/Police Force. Considering the thousands of languages in the world, adoption of a common language other than English, French, Arabic or Chinese would go a long way toward encouraging a more level "playing field" for respectful and even-handed cooperation among delegates and nations. Refer again to Appendix E. Adoption of a common (neutral) language would eliminate wrangling and complications to translate and publish proceedings as now takes place in the U.N. Adoption of an easy-to-learn neutral language also would simplify recruiting, training and command functions of the Global Peace/Police Force.

A Limited Global Government would support international courts such as those already in existence: the World Court that adjudicates disputes between nations, and the new International Criminal Court, which takes cases dealing with individuals accused of war crimes and genocide, which the U.S. has not joined. Under the umbrella of a LGG, the many agencies now affiliated with the U.N. would continue their management of normal operations between and among nations and augment efforts to eliminate poverty and promote education, health and development. The efforts of these agencies would need to be enhanced to really come to grips with world poverty, a root cause of terrorism and critical global ecological issues.

How could a Limited Global Government be funded without competing with revenue sources on which nations now depend? There are several possible sources. Revenue could be garnered from many international sources and transactions such as miniscule fees and taxes on: international financial transactions, international trade, international air tickets, and there are other sources. (For example, look up "Binding Triad" and "Tobin Tax" on the Internet.)

Until our time the idea of world government clearly was a utopian dream because technologies and communication skills were inadequate to support the complicated communication, financial and administrative machinery that would be required to maintain such an endeavor and fulfill its reason for being. Things have become very different in the last few decades. I quote a short paragraph from my *Healing the World*:

> "We are the first generations in human history with communication and technological capability to actually realize a true worldwide civilization, in all that should mean. We are the first generations with a sharpened concern for human rights and the ability to make human rights real for the entire human family!"

In a democracy "The People Are Royalty!" The people we elect are supposed to serve us, the PEOPLE! Presidents, Prime Ministers, Members of Parliament, Senators, Congressmen are all our "hirelings"! If these "leaders" are not leading toward solutions of the critical problems that are coming at us from all directions, through our voting we must "hire" other leaders who will! If government and education leaders and the media do not help us and our children learn more about these issues and encourage us to apply our ingenuity to resolve them, new leadership is needed! If religious leaders continue old divisive ways and ignore these issues, there should be changes! It's a simple (and as hard) as that.

                             *   *   *

The primary focus of this book is the issue of humans reproducing beyond the Earth's capacity to support the human family at a decent level. Any nation (the United States?) that attempts to dominate the world for the well being of its own people will institute preemptive wars that can go on and on under the guise of "terrorism". No nation can by itself provide "security" for its people. No nation alone can resolve the overpopulation, environmental, global warming, energy, war, and economic globalization issues.

GLOBAL PROBLEMS DEMAND GLOBAL SOLUTIONS! That is why a Limited Global Government is the only intelligent and adult way to address these issues. Without a global approach to solving our problems we will waste more of the Earth's limited resources and delay the time when global issues are finally taken seriously. If we do nothing or do too little or too late, we will hasten the day when civilization as we know it could crumble.

The only hope for a reasonable future for our children and grandchildren and those who will follow must come through intelligent action by adults here today to resolve the imminent crises that are on our doorstep. We must support global law and the tough actions and sacrifices that will be necessary to make it work. This is our only hope toward a reasonable future for our grandchildren and the whole human family!

PART C:
OUR FUTURE IS UP TO US!

Perhaps I am an unmitigated optimist who believes in the basic intelligence and good will of the human family. In my travels and teaching in many parts of the world I have encountered countless thoughtful, caring people, and only a few "others".

There have always been some for whom the Golden Rule means nothing. These would include scoundrels and those who think the world owes them a living. Many people must believe it is their right to have as many children as they want to, with no regard for their parenting responsibilities. There are others who, perhaps exuding religious zeal, seem to have no conscience regarding what their actions do to other individuals or the future of everyone. Problems arise especially when these latter sorts of people gain leadership posts in our governments, corporations and other institutions.

Most people do not want to "make waves" in their lives or "lead a parade" or "be president". They want to get along with family and friends and get on with their lives without bothering others, and, hopefully, without being bothered too much by others. Most people understand the need for taxes to provide community services that help everyone, but they do want their tax dollars to be spent wisely and for the common good. The converging crises of our time demand that ordinary people must become vocal and active if their basic good will and concern for the future are to make a difference in time.

Are we at a "tipping point" so a collapse of our civilization is likely? Some experts believe we are past that point. Others believe we are not—and won't be for a long time, if ever. But if we are near the "tipping point", as I think we are, what must we do? I base my hope on basic human goodness and innate human intelligence—IF people are informed! However, I believe time is running short. It is up to the PEOPLE to become serious about the issues raised and to clamor for solutions to both Equations: People-Earth and People-People. OUR FUTURE IS UP TO US!

As thinking humans, we have choices. Doing nothing also is a choice, but the disasters that can unravel the fabric of our civilization and our democracy will march on anyway. There is an alternative that derives from our ethical and religious roots and our common sense.

Part C includes a chapter that summarizes the findings of Parts A and B, a chapter on Overpopulation, and a final chapter of Conclusions and Challenge. There also is an Epilogue.

CHAPTER 9

SUMMARY OF PARTS A AND B

Summary of Part A: the "People-Earth Equation". Part A examined the People-Earth Equation and the adequacy (or not) of the Earth's basic resources to support the human family and all living forms on a sustainable basis. A present *WORLD SHORTAGE AND DETERIORATION OF ARABLE LAND* and *LOCAL LIMITATIONS OF FRESH WATER* were identified as the most critical Earth resource factors, and both of these shortages support the "Earth is Overpopulated Now" title and theme of this book. The Earth IS overpopulated now!

Except for forests as a renewable resource, there is no imminent danger of the Earth running out of *BUILDING MATERIALS*. And there *WILL ALWAYS BE ENOUGH AIR*, but the survival of Earth's living things (as we know them today) depends on eliminating local pollution, especially in and around major cities, and reducing the content of carbon dioxide and other noxious gases in the atmosphere.

From my calculations based on *arable land available* and the *calories people need each day* to be maintained in good health, I believe the Earth could provide a comfortable "western civilization" level of living on a sustainable basis for 3 1/2 and 4 billion people! This conclusion obviously has immediate ethical, religious and economic implications.

A "western civilization" average for the whole human family should not be seen as a "dream goal" but as the only humane goal that has a chance of leading us toward a sustainable and peaceful world. If we do little or nothing, more of our neighbors on this planet will slip to a subsistence way of life, and the "attitude roots" that foster the crises we face today will grow and bring our house of cards down in only a few decades.

And what are those roots? Those roots would be revealed by attitudes and beliefs such as: "Why should I change! My wife and kids and I are getting along OK." "New technologies and inventions will always be found to solve our problems." "Why should I worry about a villager in Africa or India." "It's my right to have as many kids as I want!" "My nation does not make mistakes." "Our Presidents do not lie!" "My religion shows the only way." "I'm too busy already; let the big-wigs take care of the problems!"

Perhaps we can learn from Mattie Stepanek who wrote in *Just Peace*, "Peace begins with an attitude, and an attitude is a choice" (p. 152). The statements in the above paragraph are beliefs and attitudes. They are a *choice*, and therefore they can change. Mattie is the young inspirational poet who caught the country's [and Jimmy Carter's] heart and lived to be 13 with his debilitating disease.

Things are happening fast these days. In thinking about overpopulation and the several crises that are coming at us, I am reminded of *The Twenty-Ninth Day*, written by Lester Brown in 1978. In the book's first paragraph, Brown relates the following French riddle to teach us how exponential growth can work in nature:

> "A lily pond, so the riddle goes, contains a single leaf. Each day the number of leaves doubles—two leaves the second day, four the third, eight the fourth, and so on. 'If the pond is full on the thirtieth day,' the question goes, 'at what point is it half full?' Answer: 'On the twenty-ninth day.'"

Look again at Figure 1a and think about "The Twenty-Ninth Day" riddle! Note again how long it took the human family to reach a total of 3 billion (*hundreds of thousands of years*), and note how long it took to gain *the next* 3 billion (*only 39 years*). Just like the lily leaves, populations tend to grow at exponential rates. Although the overpopulation issue does not seem to be overwhelming us at this moment it is very real and ominous. Is Earth already at the twenty-eighth day, or the twenty ninth?

Brown, a celebrated biologist, went on to explain how—in 1978—four billion humans already were putting too much pressure on "Mother Nature", on all of Earth's systems, and that the speed of destruction was accelerating. Note especially the last line of this quote from Brown in 1978:

"The deterioration of ecological systems through human abuse [and overuse] is not new. Overcutting and the subsequent decimation of forests by humans date back to the earliest civilizations in the Middle East. What is new today is the scale and speed at which biological resources are being impaired and destroyed."

Burch and Pendell told us in *Human Breeding and Survival* (1945),
"The task of freeing all the peoples of the world from war and want and fear, we submit, is chiefly that of establishing in all countries of the world a favorable relationship between population and natural resources and technical developments."

Establishing a favorable relationship between population and natural resources and technical development is easily said but not so easily done, especially on a national scale. Burch and Pendell—even in 1945—were referring to both "People-Earth" and "People-People" equations that have been mentioned several times. It is common sense that we must establish a sustainable "balance" between what humans take from the Earth and what the Earth can offer. We must adopt or invent ways for humans to work out together—as adults—the international and global ramifications of this "balance".

I have been impressed by the manner in which Al Gore has presented his powerful message about Global Climate Change as an impending catastrophe facing all humanity. The message in his book and movie is not a partisan issue, and climate change and global warming seem to be gaining the attention they deserve. But global warming is only one of several imminent crises facing humanity. Perhaps with eight years as Vice President and his deep ecological concerns Al Gore would be a good choice for President, with Barack Obama gaining experience as his VP.

Malthus, with his concerns about overpopulation was vilified in his time as a crackpot, but his basic concept is alive and well. All through history those who raise alarm about the status quo have been brushed off by those whose lives and livelihoods were to be seriously impacted. And so it is now. We who raise these issues are not "Chicken Littles". We are presenting urgent information that must not fall on deaf ears. We are presenting urgent information that *should* lead to concerted public action.

Summary of Part B: the "People-People Equation". Part B explored three aspects of the People-People Equation, the essence of which is the need for people to learn to work together to achieve the sustainable balance between the human family and the Earth. Essentially Part B is about "culture". In that exploration EDUCATION, RELIGION (and The Arts) AND LAW were considered to be the most important of our institutions for solving both People-Earth issues and People-People issues. The chapter on each of these cultural elements is summarized below.

If the Earth has too many people *now*, the question "How can the Earth's population ever be reduced?" naturally follows and has strong ethical and religious implications. I consider these in Chapter 10.

Is Intensive "Education" the Answer? Education about the impending crises is **KEY # 1**. If anything meaningful is to happen toward resolving the overpopulation and other critical issues in time, surely it must come through *education* of young people *and* adults. Education about these issues must involve our public and private schools and continuous learning throughout one's life through schooling and the media. That last point is especially important because most of the crises facing us cannot wait for another generation or two for action to be undertaken. Adults must take action now!

That will not be easy. The media and our schools reflect and teach the values of our time and institutions. And most of those who control schools and education avoid issues that would disrupt their control of people's minds and pocket books. Further, the urgency of the crises that are upon us has become generally known so recently that textbooks and school curricula have not had time to include them. However, schools and the media must take up these issues very soon to make a difference.

If our democracy is to survive, parents, our schools and governments must "educate" our children and the average citizen to pay less attention to spectator sports and entertainment and more attention to those realities that will call for decisions that will impact everyone's life in the not too distant future. If these institutional entities do not rise to the challenge, the world's brief, enriching and tantalizing experience with "democracy" will be over, at least for our time.

Education about all of the impending crises therefore, is **KEY #1**.

Can Organized Religion and Religious People really do anything about these urgent issues? I see hope here, and I believe religion is **KEY #2**. I see hope because religion is a motivating force in the lives of many, and the vast majority of the world's people consider themselves to be religious. Most belong to or identify with one of the three *great religions*, and most say they believe in God, Allah or Jehovah.

The first thing religious leaders and people of all faiths should do is to humbly acknowledge that theirs is only one of the world's many religions, and that all religions must be respected as different routes to becoming responsible, caring adults. A "creative interchange" dialogue about this might help many people to think seriously about the connection between the values their religion encourages and the values they actually live by and to relate these to the crises we face. To overcome the crises and have a chance at a good life for themselves and their progeny, the world's religious people must become a massive moral force to help overcome the ecological, social, overpopulation and economic crises that face the human family.

Organized religion must become a force for fairness in economic matters and helping the world's disadvantaged people, especially children and the millions at or near the bottom of the world's economic ladder. Our priorities should shift *from* encouraging more and more new lives to be born *to* helping those already born to have more productive and fulfilling lives.

The first ethical principle that was mentioned involves a belief choice by humans and therefore is not absolute. However, the second ethical principle is immutable. Its outcome involves the survival of the human species on Earth.

It is heartening that lately we hear that some religious leaders are making an ethical commitment to restore the Earth's systems (the "God is Green" movement) and balance the People/Earth Equation. I understand that the third part of Edward O. Wilson's new book, *The Creation, an Appeal to Save Life on Earth*, is an appeal to the "religious community" to join those who already are working to save the Earth as the home of the human family. I couldn't agree more with that thesis.

Religious leaders therefore *must* be in the educational forefront for family planning and birth control to stabilize and reduce world population. Religious leaders (and others) must emphasize that having children must include a moral and economic commitment by the parents to support each child until he or she is grown up.

Reframing and accepting both of the ethics principles touched on above, religious people and their leaders, therefore, should work together, applying the

"Golden Rule" and fulfilling the common denominator beliefs and ethics held by all religions (Appendix D).

Ignoring the critical issues will not only impact negatively the lives of parishioners and others, but will also diminish the relevance and future of the religious organizations themselves. I believe therefore that the world's religions, their leaders and their millions of devoted members are **KEY #2** to solving the overpopulation crisis and the other crises.

Law and Limited Global Government. Evidence shows how humans, steadily through the ages and with their increasing numbers, have become more secure and more creative *by increasing the areas that function under law.* Being able to function under law also helps to insulate people against tyrannical or dysfunctional leaders who occasionally take over. I believe, therefore, that **Key #3** is enlarging the area that functions under law to include the whole world.

The world has moved from clans and tribes to principalities and nations. Because of the increasing interdependence among all people and nations, nations are no longer "sovereign" in the full sense of that word and cannot provide true security for their citizens. Nations are obsolete in their inability to handle global issues and I listed reasons to support that contention.

Overpopulation and other issues touched on in this book are global issues that can be resolved only by global solutions. Air and water pollution, sharing more fairly the production of the world's farms and forests, seeking alternative energy sources, the response to global climate change, the poverty of most of the human family, and dealing with overpopulation are among these great and urgent *global* issues. Because these great moral and practical issues cannot be resolved by any single nation or a group of nations, the human family needs a Limited Global Government. It is not a dream for some time in the future. It is needed now.

The formation of a Limited Global Government, therefore, is the next crucial step. Several routes by which such a world government might come to reality have been discussed for years. In *Healing the World*, I explain three approaches by which a Limited Global Government might come into being. Very briefly these are: [1] Real reform of the United Nations (not likely). [2] A meeting of representatives of the world's people to write a Constitution for the world, to organize a Parliament of a new global government, and then to petition their governments to join. And [3] is for the world's democracies to form a Limited

Global Government and encourage people in other nations to join when stable democracies have been established.

In my view this last approach, a joining of the world's democracies, has the best chance of fulfillment in the relatively near future, whether the United States joins immediately or not. People in other democracies, following the pattern of the European Union, may be more inclined at this time to form a Limited Global Government than has been demonstrated by the government of the United States.

In poll after poll United States citizens have expressed steady support for the United Nations. U.S. citizens are well ahead of their national and state leaders who tend to be swayed by their corporate supporters. With unbiased education on global issues it is possible that the American public also would favor some kind of Limited Global Government over the virtual international anarchy that exists today.

In 1948 the voters of Connecticut voted 12 to 1 in favor of reforming the U.N. to be a real world government (*New Republic*, 12-27-48, pp 16-18), and with education it could happen again! We all are "world citizens", and the world desperately needs a democratic government of laws at the global level to help the human family deal with overpopulation and the other crises.

KEY #3 therefore is the need for global law and a Limited Global Government.

Conclusion. What else can be done to deal with the critical problems facing mankind? The United States, especially, must back away from its addiction to fossil fuels and a foreign policy dominated by bullying and war making. Money and talent released from war and preparations for war could be used for family planning education to address the global overpopulation issue. It could be better spent on developing new technologies to harness solar, wind and deep-Earth "energy slaves". Money released from military and war purposes could help stabilize and (hopefully) reverse the consequences of global warming. It could be used to rebuild long neglected public facilities and infrastructure here and abroad, to continue researching ways to reuse fresh water, to make desalinization of seawater more efficient without harming other ocean life, to abandon mega-agriculture and raise food crops on a sustainable, smaller scale and Earth-friendly basis, and to eliminate global poverty. These things can be done with a renewed human will to abandon war and establish a Limited Global Government.

CHAPTER 10

COPING WITH OVERPOPULATION

So, what can we do about the ominous fact that the Earth is already overpopulated? Can it be "fixed" in time? Rodney Shaw, President of Population Communication International stated rather bluntly in an Internet piece, "The decisions concerning the future of the world are being made in a billion bedrooms around the world each night" (<www.overpopulation.org>).

To a visitor from another planet or solar system it would appear that this human experiment on Earth, stuck as it is with outmoded nation-states, has no rational "goal" and is on a suicidal downward spiral. We are simply going along and going along as our numbers are increasing alarmingly and are about to overwhelm us. Our goal *should be* to achieve for all humans—and other living things with whom we share this planet—a reasonable quality of life that can be sustained for a very long time.

In contrast to other creatures, our evolution has brought us to be aware of ourselves and our dilemma. Evolution cannot make changes *that anticipate the future*. The process only makes mutational changes that might help the species *survive in the present*. It is up to us as intelligent, forward thinking creatures to make changes in how we do things for our own survival and future.

Regardless of other problems at hand, the special message of this book is that Planet Earth *does not* have the capacity to support all of the *present* human family at a reasonable level of living, much less the billions who are likely to be added in the years immediately ahead. And therefore, because of the limits of our Earth's bounty, world population growth must first be stopped and world population must then decline. We *are* at one of the most critical forks in the road of human history! We are in a struggle to make the momentous step from *nations* to a *global society*.

But how can the growth of the human tide be reversed in a humane fashion? What should or can we do about it? And why is the issue largely ignored in public discourse? In discussing these questions with a friend her answer was, "It is ignored because no one can do anything about it." It is another "Elephant in the Room", an obvious issue that no one wants to talk about. The human family *is* on a suicidal course. If we do nothing or too little to change that course, our human experiment on Earth will crumble in chaos within the lifetime of most people alive today.

To attack this problem we must first acknowledge that there *is* a human population problem. Then, as mentioned earlier, we must understand that nature's way has given all living things the potential to overproduce their kind, and that to survive each species must be kept in some kind of "balance" by other elements in their environment. However, "nature's way" no longer applies to humans for reasons also given earlier, and it is up to us to act.

Up to now we have ignored the overpopulation issue because of the Earth's bounty and resiliency, and we have gotten away with it. Our religions, our governments, and even our economic systems have encouraged growth, including seemingly endless population growth. However, *those days are gone and, if we are concerned about the future of our species, humans must take on the responsibility of balancing our numbers with other creatures and establish a sustainable relationship with what the Earth offers, or take the consequences.*

Serious questions come to mind: "With human (especially male) sex drives as they are can we really do anything about it at all?" "How can we deal with overpopulation humanely?" "Will or can enough of the human family through their religions, their governments, their educational systems and their good sense be able to do enough about it—in time?" "Will a couple need a license to have a baby?" (as Kenneth Boulding proposed, mentioned in Brian Czeck's *Shoveling Fuel for a Runaway Train, p.98.*) "Will women adopt the strategy (virtual bedroom locking) that Lysistrata used to end the Peloponnesian War between Athens and Sparta in the early 400s BCE", as presented in Aristophenes' play, "Lysistrata"?

Background. The overpopulation issue is not a new concern. In the late 1700s just as the Industrial Revolution was getting underway, Jonathon Swift and Thomas Malthus each wrote in different ways (one tongue-in-cheek, the other serious) about England's festering cities and population problem as they saw it. Others have carried on the concern, and in the post-WW II years there have been several books analyzing the issue. The Ehrlichs books and a few others are listed as References in the back of this book.

Probably until the middle of the 1800s birth rates and death rates around the world roughly balanced each other, with population increasing very slowly (Look again at Figure 1a.) Many children died in infancy and early childhood for a host of reasons, and the risks also were high for mothers giving birth. Successful births and childhood were celebrated because so many died very young. Risks of early death by accident or disease also were high among young people and adults. Only a small number of individuals lived to sixty and beyond, and whether one lived or died was fatalistically accepted by most as being "God's will".

Medical science has changed that by dramatically reducing the death rate through sterilization in surgery and antiseptics. Sterilization, cleanliness and medical intervention have been the primary causes of the rapid population growth in the last two centuries. With the Medical Revolution large numbers of people alive today would have "miscarried" or died in childhood and therefore would not have become parents of another generation. Nature's "natural selection" therefore no longer works with the human family. Although we are living longer, we probably are less robust as a species than in earlier times and it may be that our average cognitive ability is declining. Worldwide communication and transport, by helping to reduce mass starvation, also have been factors in the world's rapid population increase during the last century.

However, medical advances did not and can not change the basic death rate for every living thing, which remains the same as it always has been: "One death for each life", the basic and standard rate for all time! During the last century and a half the population has grown largely by increases in longevity and thus by the *delay of deaths*. After increases from longevity have stabilized, and if our attention to overpopulation and other converging crises has been successful, birth and death rates would likely again achieve a balance. However, as things are going it would be at levels even further beyond the Earth's "carrying capacity" and therefore would be unsustainable.

Relating Earth's "Carrying Capacity" To "Level of Living" As was mentioned early in this book, the overpopulation question comes down to the question *"How many people can the Earth support at a reasonable level of living on a sustainable (forever) basis?"* There can be no simple answer to that question. This is so in part because of the further question: "At whose level of living should the calculation be made as to the Earth's carrying capacity for humans?" At an average United States/ European level? At the level of living of a villager in Africa or India? Something in between?

At the near subsistence level of living of an African villager the Earth probably could support several more billions of people than it does now. *However, even that could continue for only a few more decades. Why no longer? Look again at Figure 2.* Because during those decades of world population growth the enlarging human family would make still more demands on the Earth's ecosystems, and more and more humans would slip into poverty and all of the misery it represents. In that scenario Earth's ecosystems would deteriorate further and could pass a tipping point beyond which ecosystems might be unable to renew themselves to support very many humans and other life forms. Billions of humans might die of disease and deprivation. The effects of global warming would only add to worldwide chaos and misery. When stabilization would again be achieved, the Earth might then be able to support only a few billion people, if that many.

Large populations in "western" countries are accustomed to individual freedoms, comfortable homes, reasonable diets, education, health care, vacations, some of the "finer things in life", and reasonable stability in their mostly "democratic" governments. We see these not as luxuries, but as necessities. Those who favor leaving things as they are will say the West already is aiding poorer countries enough by government "foreign aid" programs, by individuals, and through our corporations. But while we conspicuously "give" with one hand, we inconspicuously "take" with the other (probably unknowingly to most) by weakening their infrastructure and culture and leaving most of them in poverty.

Most of the billions of people around the world do not have the advantages of the "west", but they are very aware of "how the other half lives" and that these advantages are out of their reach. The "Revolution of Rising Expectations" among the poor people of the world has already been mentioned. People in "developing countries" around the world would like very much to have the West's advantages for themselves and their families. If we add the billions who desire a more fulfilling life to those who already have it, and then add each year's net increase of millions of new mouths to feed, the dire answer to the overpopulation question and the Earth's "Carrying Capacity" becomes evident.

In the sections on arable land and calories in Part A's chapter on Food it was explained how my calculations about overpopulation are based on the goal of an average "western civilization" way of life and diet for all members of the human family. This is the only humane and realistic goal if the human family is to have peace and security. But this can be achieved only if world population is reduced steadily from its present 6.5 billion people.

In the 1970s the Earth's population was about 4 billion and Lester Brown's studies concluded that the Earth's carrying capacity was the same. After my arable land and calorie calculations I initially adopted 4 billion as the target for reducing world population. However another critical factor, already alluded to, complicates the overpopulation issue.

About half of the people in developing countries are age 15 or younger. Thus, in the developing nations there are billions of children and young people coming along who will themselves have large families before any educational programs promoting birth control and stimulating economic development can be in place and begin reducing the world's population. Each person added will place an added burden on the Earth for his or her support over a lifetime. The U.N. estimates that world population may reach 8 to 9 billion by 2050 are nearly double the estimate of the Earth's 1970s "carrying capacity" of 4 billion. Perhaps Paul Ehrlich's "population bomb" already has exploded and "Day 29" is here!

Continuing population increases in the decades ahead—before birth control and family planning efforts can be effective—will contribute to further declines in the Earth's carrying capacity for people and make 4 billion a too generous target for a sustainable world's population. Adding to that unhappy prospect, these comments do not take into account the expected negative effects of global warming, which are likely to reduce still further the Earth's carrying capacity for people.

If we have honest concern for the future and how well our children and grandchildren and those who follow will live, we cannot ignore the moral imperative to balance the People-Earth Equation at about half of the world's present population.

Dealing With Overpopulation. Accepting the unhappy fact that the Earth is seriously overpopulated now, how CAN we address our overpopulation problem? How can we resolve it humanely?

There are a number of ways, but *all obviously must involve limiting the number of humans who will be conceived and born from now on.* For starters and perspective, somewhere on the Internet I read that to provide contraceptives to the vast majority of those needing them worldwide would cost $10 billions, which is about the amount spent in the United States each year on Halloween. Also, the United States is spending/wasting many lives and over $1 billion a week in Iraq.

With most of the human family less than 15 years of age, there will be at least two more decades of rapid population growth before declines can take place by any measures that might be put in place. During those decades world population is likely to increase to 7 and then 8 billion people.

Governments and religions must initiate crash programs to educate all people about the world-wide overpopulation crisis. Government programs and inducements for sterilization and to limit families to one or two children are likely to be needed. Religious attitudes or beliefs that stand in the way of world-wide family planning and birth control education and measures must be set aside as religious communities accept the reality and challenge of overpopulation and concern about the Earth.

Family planning and birth control through abstention and contraceptives are preferred ways to prevent or delay pregnancies, and with adequate pregnancy prevention, most abortions would be unnecessary. With the medical miracles available more "preemies" survive and more of us are living longer which adds to the urgency of the overpopulation issue.

Birth control and family planning education sponsored by the reformed UN (or a new Limited Global Government) and its agencies should focus on the responsibilities of parenthood and the critical role of women in birth control and family planning. Education for family planning must make the point that there is nothing grand or heroic or "macho" about simply "fathering (or mothering) a child". There should be no children until the parents are economically able and mentally ready to provide the many aspects of caring for children that are needed through the years. "Parenting is forever". It is far better to have only one or two children well cared for through their growing up years than to raise many who are likely to be disadvantaged or be a burden on society throughout their lives. It is through the care in raising children that true manliness, womanliness and adult responsibility are demonstrated.

Birth control and family planning education programs will be successful in developing countries only if accompanied by economic development to overcome the need for large families. As it is, many children provide farm helpers and "social security" in old age. With monies saved from the abandonment of war, economic development of poorer countries also would lead to economic development and political stabilization, thus helping to reduce family size and terrorism. Just as the United States did after World War II with the Marshall Plan, better off countries must increase significantly their non-military aid to developing countries, but aid should be organized only through a new Limited Global Government.

The "Ethics Conundrum". Earlier I mentioned that "attitudes" and "beliefs", as elements of human resources, could be used positively or negatively to affect how people get along in a particular place. How well or how poorly people respond to the many measures needed to address the overpopulation issue will depend on ethical beliefs about [1] birth control and abortion on one hand and, on the other, [2] human responsibility for maintaining the Earth's ability to support humans at a reasonable level of living on a sustainable (forever) basis.

Edward O. Wilson writes that "political science is the study of applied ethics" (*Consilience*, page 255). Two ethical principles touched on in the preceding paragraph are embedded in the overpopulation issue, and on the surface they appear to be in opposition. Whether these two principles are truly in opposition hinges on how each is defined and "framed" by religious leaders and others.

The **first ethic** impinging on the overpopulation issue involves the *"sanctity of life"*. To save lives has always been ethically and socially acceptable and encouraged. And medical efforts to increase longevity and reduce the death rate are applauded.

In contrast to the death rate, trying to reduce population by tampering with the birth rate evokes an opposite response. For years the U.S. government did not fund UNESCO because supposedly (and in error) it was believed UNESCO "favored" abortion. Rather than "favoring" abortion, UNESCO simply accepted the necessity and appropriateness of abortion in many situations.

The bottom line is that birth rates must come down; that is the nub of the overpopulation crisis facing humanity.

Most people who believe in the sanctity of life willingly *accept medical help to overcome illness and repair* the results of accidents, which some might construe to be interfering with God's will. On the other hand, some of these same people are against abortion and family planning because they believe humans should not interfere with God's will in *creating new life*.

Another inconsistency about the "sanctity of life" ethic is that many who proclaim the sanctity of life *before birth* and oppose abortion do not follow through with a commitment *after birth* that every child born should be sustained by caring parents, a good education and adequate health care through their growing up to assure they will be educated and healthy citizens and become caring parents during their adult years.

Some pro-life advocates say they oppose abortion because unborn babies must be accepted as "persons" from the instant of conception. Others believe "personhood" begins at birth. Still others believe "personhood" is bestowed when a child is named at 2 or 3 years of age when some aspects of his or her abilities, personality and interests may have emerged.

Perhaps part of the "sanctity of life" ethical dilemma might be resolved by acknowledging that a fetus actually is part of its Mother—and therefore cannot enjoy full personhood—until it has developed sufficiently to survive on its own after it is born. Modern medicine's capabilities to intervene successfully with "preemies" obviously complicate this last concept. But the concept of the fetus being part of the Mother until it can survive on its own might be helpful in accepting abortion as a medical procedure that relates to a woman's right to make decisions about her body.

In recent years several European countries and Russia have had stable or declining populations. And Russia recently has instituted stipends to encourage larger families. Population growth should *not* be the goal of *any* country! China and India for decades have had government programs aimed—not successfully—at limiting births to one or two children per family. New tests that can establish the sex of a fetus have complicated the abortion situation, and the practice of female infanticide still happens in countries, like China, where male-dominated cultures prevail. In many countries abortion and contraceptives are an acceptable means of family planning, whereas, in cultures with strong majorities of Roman Catholics and Muslims, and among fundamental-ist religious sects, hostility remains against use of any contraceptive or other method that might interfere with the "will of God" or the "will of Allah".

The **second ethic** derives from a deep concern about our Earth home and its ability to support all life, including humans, now and into the future. This sec-ond ethic—which looks toward the long-term survival and success of the human family on Earth—acknowledges human moral responsibility in rela-tion to the Earth that is seen and revered *as part of God's creation.* All members of the human family must adopt the role of stewards of the Earth, which we share with all other living things.

Long-term concerns for the health of the Earth's ecosystems and the Earth's "carrying capacity" for humans, therefore, are being accepted by several reli-gious denominations as an ethic of equal importance to the "sanctity of life" ethic. The "God is Green" movement among evangelicals is a case in point, and many churches are teaming up with older ecology-focused organizations whose aim is to educate the public and gain support to protect all elements of the environment.

As was noted, in a way they are. However, the "first ethic" issue is a belief and therefore a choice. The second ethic is immutable; the survival of the human species hinges on it.

Final Comments and Questions. Are these two ethics set against each other? How can one preserve the sanctity of life on the one hand and at the same time be concerned about the Earth as God's creation that must be protected for the future of all living things? Reconciliation can only come through the following: [1] pregnancy prevention so fewer abortions may be necessary, [2] acceptance of modified definitions of when human life begins, [3] acceptance of the con-cept of a Mother's rights regarding her fetus, and [4] acceptance of our ecolog-ical responsibility to take actions that will help the future of our children and grandchildren—and those who will follow. These and other measures must be presented through education, through churches and by government programs and applied worldwide if world population is to be stabilized and then reduced to match the Earth's basic fresh water and food producing resources.

From the evidence presented, it should be clear that the world already is over-populated *now* and that world population is *growing steadily.* Thus, key ques-tions arise. Is there hope that population can ever be brought down to *between*

3 ½ and 4 billion, a level at which all members of the human family could be maintained by the Earth's bounty at an acceptable level of living? Can intensive family planning and birth control make a difference in time? Is disease or war likely to significantly reduce world population? Can our religions, with reframing some of their perceptions, become major factors in helping people understand and take action on both ethical issues? Will continued increases in population soon cause a "no return tipping point" in regard to the Earth's ability to renew itself to support people at a sustainable level? How will global climate change impact the Earth's "carrying capacity" and overpopulation?

There can be no "answers" now for those questions. However, as has been stressed in this chapter, if the world's overpopulation issue and the other critical issues are to be faced realistically at all, all people and nations must face them together—and soon. Billions of couples in all countries must make difficult decisions in their bedrooms at night and during the day not to have children at all or to have only 1 or 2.

Abandoning war as a failed element in foreign policy would be the critical first step and would release substantial funds in all countries to initiate many necessary programs. A Limited Global Government is essential to galvanize and focus efforts to reduce the world's population, and to eliminate poverty and terrorism.

Will all of this lead us to a world that is vastly different from our present world? Yes, it will. But we should not be proud of our present world of war and waste, a world with the very rich and billions more very poor, a world with the continuing threat of random attack by suicidal soldiers with bombs attached to their bodies or attacks by other soldiers, including our own, piloting planes loaded with bullets and bombs. Can changes lead to a better world through intelligent and unselfish decisions by adults? A world with a Limited Global Government is achievable. A world with a smaller total population, but all of whose people are educated, healthy and caring, would be a better place to live than our present chaotic and unjust world.

We must take the positive approach—together, and get to work. But there is not much time. It is up to us what happens to this human experiment on our blue planet Earth spinning in space. Are we truly concerned about what kind of a world we will be leaving as a legacy for our children and all children?

CHAPTER 11

CONCLUSION AND CHALLENGE

We have turned away from slavery, child labor and the chattel-like status of women, all of which can be supported by this verse or that in the Bible. The Bible also tells humans to procreate and dominate the Earth on the one hand but also tells us to be humble stewards on the other. Much has been learned in all cultures since the books of the Bible were written down. We now know, as was not understood then, that instead of domination, humans must be stewards and seek a sustainable balance in our relationship with our Earth home if we are to survive as a species.

Overpopulation is another issue about which everyone needs to be very concerned for reasons that have been explained. To come to grips with the population issue in the next few years we humans will have to work simultaneously on three different but equally important tasks. [1] We must help children already born and those to be born and everyone to have lives that will be as fulfilling as possible even as they are taught about the converging crises. And they must be taught about the overpopulation crisis. [2] We must encourage parents to have only 1 or 2 children. And [3], we must make whatever difficult changes are needed to establish a sustainable balance with our Earth home.

Many studies confirm the critical deterioration of the Earth's life support systems for all living things in recent decades, but few have "connected the dots" directly with the growing human population. Lifetime learning that focuses honestly on family planning and birth control are a "must"—worldwide. And because of the Earth's limits, we must abandon the idea that growth of anything and everything "shows success". We must adopt *sustainability* as our goal. As economist Brian Czeck said in his 2000 book, *Shoveling Fuel for a Runaway Train* (p. 177):

> "Economic growth.... is a wonderful thing in its earliest stages, but its utility declines as it proceeds. At some point it becomes a bad thing—it becomes economic bloating. At that point society's grandkids depend on society to halt the process and establish a steady state economy."

Economic growth and population growth *have* become "bloated". And when Brian Czeck says grandkids must depend on "society" to halt the growth process, he means "we the people", not "somebody else". Having a sustainable relationship of humans with the Earth can be compared with living from the interest on an investment. If the burgeoning human family is using more from the Earth than what the Earth can provide on a "forever" basis—and we humans are doing just that, our Earth's ability to support humans on a long term basis is jeopardized.

The two basic needs for the sustainability of the human family on Earth are *arable land* and *fresh water*. Regardless of what happens in our oil addiction, the present and increasing population already is reducing the Earth's arable land inventory and availability of fresh water per person. Furthermore, we are not addressing the real cause of our political insecurity which relates to other critical problems. *The real causes of terrorism are poverty and hopelessness of most of the human family on the one hand and greed and indifference of so many on the other.*

Leaders of all institutions must help their members and employees toward more cooperation and sharing among the human family. If world population is ever to be stabilized and then reduced, economic development must pro-ceed—along with education—in the developing countries. Furthermore, the vast differences between rich and poor must be reduced among all of the world's people.

Throughout this book the words "crisis", "crises", "critical" and "catastrophe" have been used over and over. They have been used because they fit well with the urgency of my message, but there is danger in that. The danger is that, on being confronted with the seriousness of the overpopulation issue and the other converging issues, some people might just "tune out", give up, and "sit on the sidelines". As is clear from my writing about this at all, I am an optimist about the human family. I urge everyone to learn more about and face up to the critical issues, and then join others to make changes that will help bring on a more just future.

If we use our brains and activate our compassion to reduce our number of children, share with others and make intelligent "people and environment serving" changes, in a few decades we might all be winners. But it will not be easy. Review again items 1, 2, 6, and 7 in the "Declaration of a Global Ethic" (Appendix D2) and items 1, 3, and 6 in the list of Ethical Points from the *2005 State of the Future* (Appendix D3). A key point among these is that ecological concerns must prevail over "economic progress".

A modest decline in the level of living of the world's "better off" citizens is likely to come with actions that must be taken to face up to overpopulation and the other issues. However, we will feel better about ourselves and be more secure and better off for being healthier, less litigious, less wasteful, and more secure. With no serious attention to the converging crises, we will all be losers in only a decade or two.

It is no secret I believe a Limited Global Government is essential to deal with the *global* issues we all face. How else are we to deal with global issues other than by a global institution that has been given the power and stature to deal directly with nations? We know too well from history that one nation dominating an empire does not last very long. The idea of world government is an old idea whose time has come. The human-made catastrophe that would follow our doing nothing about the crises facing us would be of our doing, not God's. We would be mindlessly following the lemmings over the cliff.

It is tragic to think of the billions spent futilely over the centuries on armaments and military actions for the purpose of killing other people and destroying things other people have struggled to build at great cost. By abandoning war and saving the billions thus wasted, all countries could build or strengthen their democracies, their education and health programs, and carry out desperately needed infrastructure improvements in towns and cities.

If there is to be successful future for the human family, everyone must pitch in to help bring about a world of fairness and justice. Everyone can have a role to play in improving our world. Everyone can participate in this greatest of all challenges in facing up to the converging crises. And I aim that challenge especially to my grandchildren, my great-nieces and nephews, and young people everywhere who have most of their years ahead of them.

How can we do this? Here are several suggestions:

A. We must apply positive religious beliefs shared by the Great Religions and draw on the best that is in each of us to deal directly with the People-Earth Equation and the People-People Equation, both of which include the overpopulation issue.

B. We must teach our children in homes, schools and religious institutions about the critical issues that face us, and cooperate with others as we seek solutions that truly will address the issues.

C. We must abandon apathy, greed, "get rich quick" schemes and "me-firstism" and replace them with understanding, cooperation, sharing and goodwill. In doing so we will regenerate hope for a better future.

D. We must accept the hardship and sacrifices that will come with major changes as we work with those of different cultures and religions toward people-serving goals and solutions to the converging crises.

E. We must encourage all people and governments to establish a Limited Global Government so we can solve global issues between the world's people and nations as adults should—*without war.*

Already many groups, organizations and think tanks are working on some of these issues—including global government—one way or another. Information about each of these is on the Internet. I mention only a few in no particular order: "The Trilateral Commission", "Citizens for Global Solutions", "United Nations Association—USA", "Democratic World Government", "Vote World Government" (Canadian), the "World Wisdom Council", "KIVA Micro-loans", "The Forgiveness Project", the "Gorbachev Foundation", the "State of the World Forum", the "Zero Population Foundation", "Planned Parenthood", "Peace Jam", "Seeds of Peace", the "Student World Assembly", "World Population Awareness", "World Democratic Movement", and the "Foundation for Global Community".

All efforts to change our institutions and our ways of doing things come down to the need for compassion toward others. **Individuals must change** first so they can be instruments of positive change in their governments, communities and religions. There is more than a truism in the song line from yesteryear that says, "Let Peace be here on Earth, and let it begin with me". I am reminded again of Henry Nelson Wieman's **"Creative Interchange"** concept, which tells us that most creative things that humans do or have ever done are the result of

"Creative Interchange" between individuals, and he was not talking about giving birth to a child.

Any hope of the human family coming to grips with the converging crises depends on honest efforts at "Creative Interchange" between individuals at all levels of human endeavor. We cannot solve problems with the strong taking advantage of the weak (or crushing them in war); even Hammurabi's law said "No" to that a long time ago. We cannot talk past each other, with one person analyzing the problem from one point of view and the other by another approach. Creative Interchanges must be respectful, with each of those involved being truly interested in finding a fair sustainable solution to the issue.

The last of the seven points in the "Declaration of a Global Ethic" tells us: "Earth cannot be changed for the better unless the consciousness of individuals is changed first. Therefore we commit ourselves to the global ethic, to understanding one another, and to socially-beneficial, peace-fostering, and nature-friendly ways of life." (Appendix D2)

Near the end of *Healing the World* the following paragraph is in the section called "A Web of Survival":
> ".... Hope and Pride can be considered the "keys" to the accomplishment of the solution strategies.... Every person needs HOPE and PRIDE in whatever they do. Hope energizes us to accomplish our dreams. Hope inspires and, like a magnet, draws people together to work for a better tomorrow. Hope is the engine of the future. And pride helps each of us to stand tall with satisfaction over important jobs well done, especially jobs that help others and make things better for our children and those who will follow."

The 1948 Universal Declaration of Human Rights states that every person, every citizen of the world, has a right to food, water, shelter, and dignity. And having HOPE and PRIDE can go a long way toward fulfilling each person's need to live his or her life with DIGNITY.

For the United States to regain its position of respect among the world's people, we must identify values that embrace the basic good that is in all religions and people. We must accept that the best long-term interest of the human family will NOT be served by one powerful nation or by an overwhelmingly profit driven economy. Furthermore, *there are many very important ecological, com-*

munity and people needs and values that we MUST adopt and fulfill that cannot neatly fit on a balance sheet or respond to a cost-benefit analysis or a profit-driven "bottom line"! Such community needs and values are for "public profit" and are more important than the well-being of any single business enterprise. Read these last lines again.

The Importance of the Young. It is understandable that many young people and older folk have become disillusioned by constant negative campaigning, elections dominated by sound bytes, by vote count disputes and the obvious eroding "health" of our democracy in recent years.

Senator Paul Simon, among his many interests, was keenly interested in having an effective U.N. He was dismayed that most young people, perhaps jaded by the media's criticisms of the U.N., seemed to have little interest in the U.N. or how to make it more effective. **Gillian Sorenson**, formerly on the U.N. staff, visited Southern Illinois University in Carbondale on U.N. Day in October 2006 and presented a stirring address to an overflow crowd who gave her a standing ovation at its close. In her address, she **echoed Paul Simon's concern and urged the hundreds of young people who were in attendance to study the U.N. and world affairs and to work for changes that will lead toward a better world for all.**

Toward the end of *An Inconvenient Truth* Al Gore made a profound observation: "Political will is a renewable resource". In this book I have noted "attitude" as a "human resource". **Political will to do what is right for the common good IS a renewable resource, but it can only be built on HOPE, the engine of tomorrow, and hard work by the PEOPLE!**

Very simply: "It IS Up To Us", those **who are here NOW, to make a difference!** Young and older, we are the ones who are here and alive in this time of converging crises. We must not ignore the issues and let things go on as they are. We must work as individuals and together as **"World Citizens" to resolve the "People/People Equation" and the "People/Earth Equation"**, two challenging equations that must be solved if our children and grandchildren are to have a reasonable future.

And who will lead this marvelous, exciting and necessary journey to a better future? Who will pick up the many challenges that have been raised? I hope the younger readers of this book and my earlier one will take up the challenge. And I hope that among those picking up the gauntlet will be younger leaders like **Al**

Gore, Barack Obama, Dick Durbin, Bill and Hillary Clinton, Dennis Kucinich, John Edwards, Sheila Simon, Nick Scala, Jane Fonda, Bill and Melinda Gates, Robert Redford, Helen Caldicott, Jack Stewart, Ted Turner, Richard Whitney, and Jan Schakowsky who already have demonstrated interest in government *for the people* and in some of the key issues of our time.

Inspired leaders will gather and organize a non-violent army of enthusiastic young and older folks. Members of this enthusiastic army will want to see their lives have real purpose in helping make David Korten's **"Great Turning"** and some kind of "World Community" and **global government** become reality. They will want to work on behalf of a better future for a smaller number of humans working together on our **"blue-green spaceship"**, as Bucky Fuller used to call the **Earth, the human family's only home.**

EPILOGUE
(ESPECIALLY FOR CITIZENS OF
THE UNITED STATES)

Even as we have made many marvelous discoveries and impressive technological advances over the years, we humans also have bumbled around the Earth
and have undercut the Earth's ability to support our enlarging human family.
Our future as a species is in the balance. The hyper-individualism and blind
"patriotism" of United States' citizens, the skewed teaching of our history, our
fetish with religion and religiosity, our misguided view of the marvels of the
"market economy", and our male-dominated way of life have brought "western
civilization" to the edge. Because of several "cultural blocks" the United States
especially is blocking ourselves and others from attending to the survival of the
human species.

An Epilogue is in order to add further insights I have gleaned from additional
reading since completing my manuscript for *Earth is Overpopulated Now*.
Years ago I was aware of Jared Diamond's *Guns, Germs and Steel* and books
about the prevalence and prominence of goddesses in the human past.
However, being busy with family and many other things as so many of us are, I
did not assimilate them. I am in awe of the range and depth of the research and
findings in these books. Their messages are clear and critically relevant in rela-
tion to the converging crises.

In this Epilogue I try to accomplish two things: 1. To explain why I think we
must take the messages of these books very seriously in our dealing with the
crises that face us in these early years of the twenty-first century. 2. To intro-
duce the term "cultural block" and list the several "cultural blocks" I see in the
United States' present culture as well as how we can overcome them. I also
recap why the organization of a Limited Global Government is essential to
overcome the converging crises, especially overpopulation.

Three Books About Goddesses and "Empire". Merlin Stone's 1976, *When God Was a Woman* weaves a well-documented explanation about very early times in the experience of humans on Earth. It was a time when men and women, for their survival, were partners in doing everything and how, learning from nature and human birthing, fertility and growth were understood, goddesses were worshipped, and women participated in group leadership.

Riane Eisler's 1987 epic, *The Chalice and the Blade*, carries Stone's story along with more details that have been building from archeological works since World War II. Eisler divides the early history of humankind into two eras. The earlier, which lasted for most of the last 200,000 years, she calls *"partnership"*, and it follows the story of early humans and goddess worship that Stone had written about so persuasively. Eisler's later era, which came with the Agricultural Revolution about 8000 BCE, she calls *"domination".* The "Domination era, a male-dominated way of life, has persisted until the present. This male-dominated way of life ignores (and has virtually obliterated) the earlier "goddess history" and has fashioned all of our institutions—worldwide—to reinforce male dominance. Eisler writes (page xv) that we are at an "evolutionary crossroad" and that "war and the 'war of the sexes' are neither divinely nor biologically ordained." Her "chalice and blade" metaphors were used in the book and movie, *The DaVinci Code.*

In 1996 Mark Woodhouse wrote *Paradigm Wars: Worldviews for a New Age.* In it he identifies a number of principles that have shaped the current Western worldview: fragmentation, reductionism, competition, hierarchical control, and fear. He goes on to explain how these *principles of male domination* "have led us to crises of such magnitude that we can survive only by abandoning (those) ways of thinking and behaving that have brought us to the brink" (p. xiii). He goes on in his book to consider the more "inclusive metaphors of integration, balance, (multidimensional) wholeness, mutually empowering cooperation, and love" as approaches that might point our civilization in a new and more hopeful direction. He also explores many topics—time, psychology, education, religion and the galaxy—as he seeks a new vision for our time.

In the earlier pages of this book I mentioned David Korten's important book, *The Great Turning* (2006), which draws from and follows Eisler's theme from *The Chalice and the Blade.* Korten explains that the challenge and opportunity of our time is to shift away from our worldwide 5000 year old male-dominated culture (that Korten calls *"Empire"*) and reestablish the earlier concept with a male-female balance in all activities that Eisler calls *partnership* and Korten calls *"World Community"*. The realization of **partnership** of the sexes and **world community** are desperately needed in our time and are keys to dealing with the converging crises.

According to Eisler and Korten, during the earlier 200,000 years of our human pre-history, men and women worked together as equals in their families, clans, tribes and villages. Besides survival, animistic religion and making a living by hunting and gathering were major concerns. The whole way of life was tuned to learning about and using nature's bounty for survival and trying to deal with the sometimes violent natural forces. Their simple ways and small numbers did not upset the "balance of nature". Their deities were goddesses, and—with evidence all around them—their religion focused on nature and fertility.

Contrary to the way much of history is taught, Eisler also presents evidence that technological developments of considerable sophistication and importance were made by human communities in many parts of the world long before the Agricultural Revolution and the advent of Korten's male-dominated "Empire".

"Empire" came about 8000 to 5000 years ago with the Agricultural Revolution, the adoption of "planting". This brought the shift *from* an Earth-oriented way of life and balance between the sexes *to* the male-dominated "Empire" that has persisted to this day. Male-domination set aside goddess veneration, brought on an array of hierarchical institutions, a wealthy elite, and highly competitive ways of life. In contrast to the pre-Empire ages, the male-dominated way tends toward confrontation, war and violence in futile efforts to solve problems. And the level of violence has increased with population growth, increased pressure on the Earth's natural resource base, and as more lethal weapons are invented. Korten sees the urgent need for a "Great Turning" in our time from "Empire" to an "Earth Community".

Korten asserts very persuasively that all institutional forces in the male-dominated cultures around the world are still keeping most PEOPLE, male and female, from growing beyond a teenage "me first", "my way", and "to win!" mentality and attitude. He says the educational process and the economic systems of the industrialized "developed" world do not help most humans achieve the fullness of their potential. Education does not include enough concern for the success of the whole human family and an understanding of our utter dependence on the Earth's bounty.

Korten says (pages 25–26),

> "The defenders of Empire teach that we humans are by nature limited to a self-centered and ultimately self-destructive narcissism. Their favored organizing model suppresses development of the higher orders of human consciousness and thereby creates a self-fulfilling prophecy. The organizing model of Earth Community, by contrast, nurtures expression of the higher-order human capacities for responsible service that Empire denies. A convergence of imperative and opportunity unique to the present moment in the human experience sets the stage for an intentional collective choice to put the way of Empire behind us as we live into being a new era of Earth Community."

Cultural Blocks. Jared Diamond's 1997 *Guns, Germs and Steel* notes that different cultures have reached points which seem to block them from moving on, and for decades in my geography classes I taught about what I called "cultural blocks". One example I have used is the imprecise Chinese written language that is comprised of over 60,000 pictorially derived characters, a language that has evolved over thousands of years. Most Chinese know a few thousand characters, and only a few have mastered most of that enormous vocabulary. However, even with their complex language, the Chinese led the world in technological advances during the Tang Dynasty from 618 to 906 CE. Since it opened to western trade and influences in the late nineteenth century, China has caught up with the rest of the world technologically. There have been repeated efforts to modify the Chinese language with an alphabet of simplified characters and romanizstion, even drawing on Esperanto and English.

A second example of a cultural block is the very limited and complex Roman numeral system. The Roman system, with its I, V, X and other letters and notations, was basically for addition and subtraction. It was very limited in dealing with fractions and, with no zero, did not lend itself for serious mathematical advancement. It was used in Europe until the 900s and was adequate to facilitate Rome's military and empire building and its impressive architectural and other engineering feats.

A third example I used is drawn from *Shipwreck and Empire*, written by James Duffy (1955). Its main theme is about the rise and fall of Portugal's empire. This small country at the southwest corner of Europe was the first in Renaissance times, under the leadership of Prince Henry, to explore the world by water. Portugal's ships sailed around Cape Horn, at Africa's southern tip, to India, east through the islands of Southeast Asia, and then as far north as

Nagasaki, Japan. They also sailed as far west as San Salvador, Brazil. The Portuguese were first to develop a colonial empire, using ponderous ships, called carracks and galleons. Dutch and English mariners finally built smaller ships that could out-maneuver Portugal's fleets and more easily get into and out of ports. In the last years of Portugal's struggle to maintain its prominence and empire many of their ships were overloaded, poorly repaired and more subject to damage or shipwreck from storms that are common around Africa's southern tip. Partly because of their ponderous ships, the Portuguese, with Spain to follow after the defeat of its Armada, finally lost out to England in empire building and its early domination of the world.

The United States and "Cultural Blocks". In context of the *"cultural block"* concept, I look at the United States and believe our country is "blocked" from joining with and moving ahead with the rest of the world in the twenty-first century by two sets of realities. One of these relates to the growing power of wealthy individuals and corporations and our election process. These are blocking progress toward fulfilling the "American Dream" and the actual attainment of 'liberty and justice for all" citizens.

By design of the Founding Fathers, ours is a "winner take all" electoral system by which those elected are supposed to act on behalf of the common good of all citizens. However, with only narrow majorities it is possible for one political party to dominate the "affairs of state" for years, with no recourse by the public at large.

Electoral corruption and collusion surely happened in state and national electoral processes since the United States' beginnings. However, the opportunity for mischief and manipulation has been magnified in recent decades by the introduction of computerized voting machines, the bitter, lengthy and increasingly expensive campaigning, and the power of the media, especially television. In recent decades the media has been co-opted by the "military-industrial complex" which, through campaign contributions and lobbying, now virtually owns the White House, our Congress and state legislatures. Voter apathy and distrust of government are cynical byproducts of these manipulations that block reasonable progress toward a more fair and just society.

A second "cultural block", related to our media and even to religion, also interferes with the United States functioning as a community of citizens seeking to fulfill the American Dream. Our educational system, in all of its public and private manifestations, and our religions, do not help our children and young people to develop skill in *evidence-based thinking*. Children and young people grow up too prone to believe what they are told by "authorities". As has been noted elsewhere in this book, *evidence-based thinking and decision making* by an informed electorate is essential for the health and survival of a democracy.

For over two centuries we were insulated from the rest of the world and its troubles by two oceans. Especially since World War II communications and transportation inventions have neutralized that insulation. We now are held back from dealing reasonably with other nations by feelings of superiority that stem from our history and the power of our military, the media and our economy. The myopia of our educational system and our dominant religions is not preparing our children and young people to deal fairly with other "world citizens" who have different religions and cultures. We must overcome both of these cultural blocks and rejoin the world!

As a final observation about cultural blocks that interfere with the United States moving ahead in these early years of the twenty-first century, a comparison may be made with the Roman Empire. The United States is much like the Roman Empire in terms of the predominance of the military in our budgets, our foreign policy, and the unquestioned acceptance of such a powerful military by many citizens. There may also be similarity in Rome's providing diversionary games in the Coliseum and in the way television, games and entertainment divert American citizens from close attention to the diversionary military strikes and small wars that are being perpetrated around the world in our name. We should not forget what happened to Rome. Despite its structure of democracy along with a Senate, Rome did not survive its string of bad and even not-so-bad dictators.

A New Political Party in the U.S.? Much of what needs to be done about these many issues will take political action *by the people*, and I see the need for a **new political party in the U.S.** An alternative would be for a party now in existence to add "planks" to their platform that focus honestly on the realities of our time. And the new party—or revitalized old party—must be accompanied by a complete reform in how our elections are managed and how votes are counted!

With the baggage of their history and organization, I see little prospect that either the Republican or Democratic Party can be reformed to take on the challenge. Perhaps the Green Party might be challenged to broaden its agenda. Already the Green Party's platform targets environmental and other elements of the converging crises. If the Green Party were to add concern for the overpopulation issue, support for Global Cooperation and Global Government to their platform they might find a very receptive citizenry and become that new party.

If the Green Party is unwilling to do this, then a brand new political party is needed, even as we acknowledge that the process by which a new political party may be organized and accepted in the U.S. is a bureaucratic minefield. A new party is justified by the negative campaigning and virtual stalemate of the two major parties in the U.S. to face up to important issues. And that new party could attract young voters who do not want their years ahead to be wasted and their democracy to be compromised.

The new party's platform should include the following ten points:

1. **Protect the environment from further damage and deterioration.** Pass needed laws that will be phased in over a few years so individuals and businesses can make needed changes to accommodate sustainable practices. "Harmony with nature is more important than economic progress." (Appendix D3, item 1)

2. **Support birth control education and accept necessary abortions.** Abortion should be a pregnant woman's right in all cases up to full term. These measures are absolutely essential if we are to make progress in reducing the world's population.

3. **Support research and development of technologies that will address critical issues.** These must include: energy alternatives, global warming, fresh water needs and agricultural conversion to smaller, Earth-friendly types of farming that can be sustained.

4. **Support progressive taxes and inheritance reform.** It is foolish to leave the masses of citizens to pay for (foolish) actions or programs that benefit only the wealthy, businesses, corporate leaders and shareholders. Progressive taxation with very few exceptions must be adopted. A democracy can survive only with modest differences in levels of income among the people and with no massive estates being handed down for generations.

5. **Support government-provided education and health care for all citizens.** The most effective security for all individuals and democratic governments will come through an informed and healthy citizenry who share a level of living that has limited extremes. Those with special abilities should

be supported through college. And health care should be through a universal single payer system administered by the government.

6. **Institute public funding of campaigns and modify voting laws and procedures so only *VOTERS* can contribute to campaigns (NOT corporations, unions or other organizations)!** The "separation of church and state" was wisely built into our government by our Founding Fathers. But the United States now desperately needs effective campaign financing laws *to separate our government and the election process from lobbyists, the influence peddling and dominance by wealthy individuals and corporations!*

7. **Designate election days to be national holidays and make other changes in election procedures.** Paper ballots must back up every election. "Instant Runoff Voting" should be adopted for more fairness in voting, especially for minorities. As is done in Europe, limit campaigns and campaigning to 60 or 90 days before an election (the media would not like this!). The archaic "Electoral College" should be eliminated. Voting districts should be compact, not gerrymandered.

8. **Misguided precedents have been cited repeatedly following the erroneous labeling on May 10, 1886 of a Supreme Court decision. The error was used to give corporations the same rights and advantages in the law that "persons" have.** These should be reversed. Despite legal gobble-de-gook, corporations do not die and are not people, and corporate money is NOT the same as free speech.

9. **Support efforts to organize an independently funded Limited Global Government to address global issues on a global basis.** Such efforts must include a replacement of national military establishments (and the world's trillion dollar a year military bill) with a new volunteer Global Police/Peace Force. Development of a Global Police/Peace Force must parallel an orderly and phased disarmament in all countries down to levels needed for internal security.

10. **Lead (but not dominate) efforts through the Limited Global Government to provide worldwide assistance to those hopelessly trapped in poverty.** By such efforts and cooperating with others, the U.S. would regain its position of respect among the world's people. "Terrorism" would recede and all nations and people would be more secure.

Final Words about a Limited Global Government. Despite the need for some kind of "World Community" presented in the several books noted (Diamond, Korten, Eisler, Woodhouse, and the Ehrlichs), none acknowledges and presents the next logical and necessary step for the human family to achieve a world—*with* cooperation and *without* war—that can face up to the male-dominated "Empire" and the coming crises. "World community" **must** be based on a Limited Global Government with "global law".

And note I use the term "global law", not "international law". This is very important. The next level of law must be global and *above* the nations, not just between nations, as the term "*inter*national law" implies. *The point can be well understood when we acknowledge that laws coming from the federal government in Washington are much more than "interstate laws"!*

Tinkering by nations with this or that problem cannot do enough. The *first* necessary step to come to grips with overpopulation and other critical issues is the establishment of a Limited Global Government by a joining of the world's people. Without such a government over the nations, we will continue the same ways that have brought us the League of Nations and the United Nations and have brought our so-called "civilization" to the brink of collapse. Without a global government the world will engage in more wars and waste the world's last barrels of crude oil as nations struggle with the converging crises and the results of overpopulation.

I have no illusions that a finely tuned and workable Limited Global Government can be organized and in operation in the next few years. Adults everywhere must first come to realize that war never was and surely is not now an intelligent adult way to solve problems between nations. War is obsolete. And, yes, it will be difficult to dismantle the war machines of the nations unless an effective Global Peace/Police Force and a plan for disarmament have been agreed upon and is in place.

With PEOPLE POWER pushing for it, a workable Limited Global Government could be organized in about ten years and be functioning reasonably in the next ten. The political WILL is what is needed! The U.N. Charter was written and the U.N. was organized in less than a year, but in 1945 only about 50 nations, mostly European and "Western" were involved. It will not be easy now with 191 "nations" that range in size from a few thousand people to 1.4 billion.

With the support of government, religious and other leaders, the Internet and the media, people *can* be taught what is at stake and to support a Limited Global Government, either by true reform of the U.N. or by another approach. People in other countries are far more ready for such discussions than citizens of the U.S. citizens appear to be. As Korten says, the PEOPLE must learn about and push for and become part of "The Great Turning"—which IS coming with or without human planning.

Through the Limited Global Government we can abolish war and work together to address the overpopulation issue and eliminate endemic poverty everywhere, the principle root of terrorism. To eliminate poverty we must increase economic opportunity in ways that have been suggested, spread the word about family planning, and thus slowly but surely reduce the world's population. Good people of all faiths must reconcile the two ethics I have identified.

All people must engage their consciences and attach the star of their driving beliefs to cooperate with other people balance the two Equations (the "People/Earth Equation" and the "People/People Equation"). We must do this—together—if we are to achieve a better life for our grandchildren and for the entire human family. And it must be a better life and life system that the Earth can sustain forever.

David E. Christensen
November 2006

CIRCLES OF CARING

By ignorance and tinkering
    our world is dying.
By violence, war and greed
    "civilization" is slipping from us.
By arrogance and blindness
    brief experiments with democracy
    may be ending—again.

Too many think only of power and profit.
Ears and eyes are closed to the plight
    of our neighbors on this planet.
The Circle of Caring is broken.

Too many think only of power and profit.
Eyes and ears are closed to the distress
    of our Earthly home, our only home.
The Circle of Stewardship is broken.

Must it be? Must it be?
Only through strong voices, stronger actions
    and working together
    can the Circles be repaired,
      … if already it is not too late.

It is up to us
    to awaken to these truths.
It is up to us
    to join with others in voice and action.
It is up to all of us,
    on behalf of the human family
      and those yet unborn,
    to be catalysts for a fairer world,
      restoring the Earth and ourselves
      under global law.

    David E. Christensen / June 2006
    (Mostly written at a poetry workshop at
    the Unitarian-Universalist Association
    General Assembly in St. Louis, MO)

APPENDICES

APPENDIX A: SOME (MOSTLY OLDER) BOOKS ABOUT "PEOPLE-EARTH ISSUES"

Among the books that have carried this clarion call are: Paul B. Sears, *Deserts on the March* (1935); William Vogt, *Road to Survival* (1948): Fairfield Osborn, *Our Plundered Planet* (1948) and *The Limits of Growth* (1953); Vernon Gill Carter, *Man on the* Landscape (1949), Samuel H. Ordway, *Resources and the American Dream* (1953); Tom Dale and Vernon Gill Carter, *Topsoil and Civilization* (1955); Georg Borgstrom, *The Hungry Planet* (1965); Paul Ehrlich, *The Population Bomb (1968)*, D. Meadows, D. Meadows, J. Randers, W. Behrens, *The Limits of Growth* (Reporting a "Club of Rome" study, 1972); Paul and Anne Ehrlich, *The Population Explosion* (1990), Al Gore, *Earth in the Balance* (1993) and *An Inconvenient Truth* (2006).

APPENDIX B: EXCERPTS FROM *2005 STATE OF THE FUTURE* AND U.N. MILLENNIUM DEVELOPMENT GOALS

B1. Excerpts from Executive Summary of *2005 State of the Future*, by Jerome C. Glenn and Theodore J. Gordon, pages 1-4.)

"Just as it would be difficult for the human body to work if the neurons, muscles, bones, and so on were not properly connected, so too it is difficult for the world to work if people, ideas, resources, and challenges are not properly connected.... Yet the moment-by-moment connectivity among ideas, people, resources and challenges in order to create optimal solutions is yet to be developed. A worldwide race to connect everything not yet connected is just beginning, and great wealth will be made by completing the links among systems by which humans and civilizations function and flourish ...

"This year's annual military expenditures will reach $1 trillion, and annual income for organized crime has passed $2 trillion. Yet the world has not dedicated the resources needed to stop water tables from falling, to narrow the rich-poor gap, or to provide safe and abundant energy.

"Explosive economic growth over the previous decades has led to dramatic increases in life expectancy, literacy, and access to safe drinking water and sanitation and to decreases in infant mortality for the vast majority of the world. Yet without the creation and implementation of a strategic plan for a global partnership between rich and poor that uses the strength of free markets with rules based on global ethics, disparities could grow and trigger increased migration of the poor to rich areas, resulting in a range of complex conflicts and humanitarian disasters. The ratio of the average income of people in the top 5% to the bottom 5% has grown from 6 to 1 in 1980 to over 200 to 1 now. This is not sustainable....

"The (year 2000) Millennium Ecosystem Assessment found that 60% of our life-support systems are gone or in danger of collapse. The assessment was conducted by 1,360 experts from 95 countries who produced a global inventory of the state of our ecosystems and warned that this degradation could grow worse by 2050 by another 2.6 billion people added to the earth. Declarations from world leaders about sustainable development have not led to actions sufficient to change this trend. Current absorption capacity of carbon by oceans is about 3 to 3.5 billions tons per year. Yet today 7 billion tons are added to the atmosphere annually, which could increase to 14 billion tons per year if current trends continue—eventually leading to greenhouse effects beyond the ability of humans to control....

".... It seems that the UN Millennium Development Goal of cutting poverty in half between 2000 and 2015 may well be met on a global basis, but not in the poorer areas in sub-Saharan Africa, and that hunger and water scarcity will continue to increase unless more serious and intelligent investments are made.

"Meanwhile, water supply has to be increased, not simply redistributed. Despite improved access to safe drinking water and better sanitation during the last decade, 1.1 billion people still to not have access to safe drinking water and 2.6 billion people—half the population in developing countries—lack adequate sanitation.

"Nearly 15% of the world is connected to the Internet, and the digital gap is closing. Millions share ideas and feelings with strangers around the world, increasing global understanding. Google and other search engines have made much of the world's knowledge available, which helps to provide a more even playing field for the future knowledge economy.... Civilization is also becoming increasingly vulnerable to cyber-terrorism, power outages, information pollution (misinformation, pornography, junk email, media violence) and to virus attacks, both electronic and biological. Weapons of mass destruction are still stockpiled and form a threat that has yet to be addressed realistically.

"By conventional definitions, most people continue to live in democracies or partly free conditions rather than autocracies. Yet in 2004 only 17% of the world's people lived in countries that enjoyed a free press.

"The world is slowly beginning to realize that improving the political and economic status of women is one of the most cost-effective ways to address the other 14 global challenges described in Chapter 1. Yet, on average, women still get paid 18% less than men, and male violence to woman causes more casualties than wars do.

"It is time for an international campaign to develop a global consensus for action against transnational organized crime, which has grown to twice the size of all military budgets combined and is increasingly interfering with governments' ability to act.

"World energy demand is forecast to increase by 60% from 2002 to 2030 and to require about $568 billion of new investments every year to meet that demand. Oil production is declining among the major producers.... Of all the decisions that face society, what would be clearer than the need for a massive Apollo-like program to increase the world's supply of non-polluting energy?

"Global ethics are emerging from a variety of sources such as the International Organization for Standardization (there are 15,036 ISO standards), corporate ethics indexes, multi-religious dialogues, UN treaties, the Olympics, the International Criminal Court, NGOs, Internet blogs, and the international news media. Ethical decision making in a globalizing world should be informed by understanding of the 15 Global Challenges described in Chapter 1 and their interconnectedness. The establishment of the eight UN Millennium Development Goals was a giant step in this direction. The next should be the creation of global transinstitutions for water, energy, AIDS, education, and so on rather than just relying on current institutional structures that are not getting the job done ... In addition to the morality and social benefits of addressing these goals and challenges, there is also great wealth to be made, as the markets for their resolution are huge and long term. However, making this more likely will require future-oriented politicians, which in turn will require a better educated public to elect more global future-minded leaders."

B2. Fifteen "Challenges" from *2005 State of the Future*, page 10.

1. How can sustainable development be achieved for all?
2. How can everyone have sufficient clean water without conflict?
3. How can population growth and resources be brought into balance?

4. How can genuine democracy emerge from authoritarian regimes?

5. How can policymaking be made more sensitive to global long-term perspectives?

6. How can the global convergence of information and communications technologies work for everyone?

7. How can ethical market economies be encouraged to help reduce the gap between rich and poor?

8. How can the threat of new and reemerging diseases and immune microorganisms be reduced?

9. How can the capacity to decide be improved as the nature of work and institutions change?

10. How can shared values and new security strategies reduce ethnic conflicts, terrorism, and the use of weapons of mass destruction?

11. How can the changing status of women help improve the human condition?

12. How can transnational organized crime networks be stopped from becoming more powerful and sophisticated global enterprises?

13. How can growing energy demands be fulfilled safely and efficiently?

14. How can scientific and technological breakthroughs be accelerated to improve the human condition?

15. How can ethical considerations become more routinely incorporated into global decisions?

B3. Eight U.N. MILLENNIUM DEVELOPMENT GOALS, from "Millennium Development Goals: Charting progress toward a better world", a map-poster developed by the World Bank, the U.N. and the United Nations Foundation, 2005.

1. Eradicate extreme poverty and hunger.

2. Achieve universal primary education.

3. Promote gender equality and empower women.

4. Reduce child mortality.

5. Improve maternal health.

6. Combat HIV/AIDS, malaria and other diseases.

7. Ensure environmental sustainability.

8. Develop a global partnership for development.

APPENDIX C: ALTERNATIVE ENERGY SOURCES

Biomass, Methane, Biogas. Because of depletion of fossil fuels and rising prices, biomass to generate electricity and to provide "ethanol" fuel for vehicles, has gotten the attention of the public and politicians as an energy "alternative". The photosynthesis process obviously can produce vegetative matter in almost all of the Earth's environments. Photosynthesis works but has its limits and cannot be hurried.

When it was first conceived, it was anticipated that biomass would provide a use for many kinds of vegetative waste materials, like the bagasse waste from production of sugar that comprises 95% by volume of the sugar cane. Since the late 1990s Brazil has become a major user of sugar cane biomass for producing ethanol.

However, food crops also are directly used as biomass raw material to make ethanol, and Brazil also makes some ethanol directly from sugar, depending on the market situation. Ethanol production in the U.S. is based largely on corn and soybeans, thus competing very directly with use of these crops for livestock production, direct food uses for humans, or for production of various chemicals. Although gasoline mixed with 10% or 85% ethanol is available at gas stations especially in the U.S. Midwest, the total "energy cost" of Ethanol's production is greater than the amount of energy the finished product can deliver.

Poverty also is a factor in the availability of potential biomass materials. Poor people in developing countries struggle and scrounge for wood, brush or dung to burn as cooking fuel, contributing to deforestation and erosion and eliminating potential soil enriching material.

In 1979 my wife, two daughters and I were shown around a small dairy farm in India where the owner/operator had harnessed the methane gas given off by animal wastes from farm owner's small dairy herd. Because of the climate he and his family did not need the gas for heating their small house, but it was important and appreciated to supply enough for their cooking needs, even though it diverted use of manure that might have been put back onto the land or as dung patties used directly for cooking.

Operators of large and small dairy and livestock farms in the U.S. also are adopting techniques to produce methane (Biogas) from animal wastes. On dairy, beef and pork farms we now might see huge round-topped "Anaerobic

Digesters" as farmers are taking advantage of animal waste materials as a "renewable resource" from their herds. Capturing methane puts it to use and keeps it from rising to intensify the "Greenhouse Gas" problems. Some farms produce more power than they can use and sell gas to local utilities to generate electricity. Early in 2006 the news informed us that a single cow's one-day production of manure generates enough Biogas to power an auto for 15 miles!

By-products from the production of biogas are a liquid effluent that *can* be used as fertilizer, and dried "sludge" that can be used as a soil conditioner, to make particle board, or to generate steam to produce electricity.

Solar Power. Solar power is the most pervasive, dependable and unlimited resource that is available all over the Earth. It is no surprise, given the many ways in which humans from their beginnings have depended on the sun, that Pharaoh Akhenaton, who ruled Egypt from 1346 to 1332 BCE, set aside Egypt's ancient pantheon of gods and in their place adopted the sun, Aton, as the one god of Egypt's religion. Other early human groups also worshipped the sun as the giver of light and life. (Akhenaton's reign was short and at its close Egypt went back to the earlier pantheon of gods.)

Since very early times the Greeks, Romans and Chinese used magnifying glasses and mirrors to light fires and torches. Passive solar heat was used for heating a home in Italy in about 100 CE. And in 6th century post-Roman Italy, the Justinian Code specified that no shadows may interfere with sunlight reaching homes and public buildings. Attention to solar energy thus has been on the human agenda for a long time.

It has been calculated that enough energy from the sun reaches the Earth to supply all possible human and other needs indefinitely. It is calculated that between 30 degrees north and south, the sun delivers an average of 2000 kilowatt hours of energy to each square meter at the top of Earth's atmosphere in a year. Only about half of that reaches the Earth's surface.

Estimates are that all human energy uses could be provided by only a few percent of the sun's total energy that reaches the Earth. This energy is not evenly bestowed. There is the obvious difference between night and day in the availability of solar power, and there are great differences between equatorial tropics and the Arctic and Antarctic areas in terms of the angle at which solar energy is received, and therefore the effectiveness of the energy delivered. And each of these presents a challenge to the generation of solar power and its transmission to provide the wide range of energy needs of all living things on Earth.

Despite the taming of fire, the harnessing of rivers, the many uses of wood, and the incidental use of reflected sunlight, attention to actually harnessing the energy power of the sun on a large scale did not become a subject for serious researchers until the Industrial Revolution was well under way. Between 1860 and the First World War inventors in France and England experimented with various means to harness solar energy. However, in spite of gathering much information and some success in developing solar powered engines, little came of it in the U.S. until after the oil shortages of the early 1970s.

Since then research has continued, even though it flagged for two decades while the petroleum giants and U.S. auto makers sold the American people on vans, SUVs and Humvees and made it appear that our oil addiction could go on forever. Following the 1970s oil shortages Europe and Japan made changes and now use energy twice as efficiently as we do in the United States.

With the imminent decline in petroleum supplies and price escalation, research for alternative energy sources has gained public support. After six years in office President Bush finally mentioned our country's "oil addiction" in his State of the Union Address in January 2006, but he made no significant suggestions for reducing the oil addiction.

The Internet tells us that research in recent decades has developed some alternatives that are competitive with conventional fuel sources. Japan has no oil resources, and since the oil crisis in the early 1970s virtually all of its increases in energy production and use have been provided from solar sources. A few years ago 30% of Israeli homes produced their hot water from solar panels; all new homes must now include solar hot water equipment. Passive solar heating also is common in Israel.

Israeli firms manufactured several groups of solar power generators that have been installed in California's Mojave desert. These have been operating efficiently since the late 1980s, and California is contracting with Israeli firms to build more efficient solar facilities to realize its goal of producing 17% of its energy by alternative sources by 2017. New solar power generators using parabolic collectors can produce electricity (in 2006) at ten cents a kilowatt hour. An even larger and reputedly more efficient solar project is underway in Nevada, using technologies developed in Germany.

The Internet also informs us that Israel developed a successful technique to produce hydrogen. Solar power and charcoal break down zinc oxide to a powder. The zinc oxide powder in turn is used to separate hydrogen from water and in the process, zinc is reformed. The hydrogen is then burned to generate electricity. A massive project in Israel's Negev Desert using this technique that is projected to provide all of Israel's energy needs by 2012.

It has been further calculated that every state in the United States could produce much of its energy needs from 17 square miles of panels using currently available photo-voltaic cell technology, even with that technology operating at only 15% efficiency. As "over-optimistic" as this might be, the information (from the Internet) is included to underscore the possibilities that may be available using current technology, and the technology is steadily improving!

The Earth's desert areas could become important in a new solar energy age. A broad band of desert and semi-desert extending across Africa from the countries of Western Sahara and Mauritania at the west end of the Sahara across Saudi Arabia, through the Near East to Western India is a region high in solar energy all year. Even after its petroleum has been depleted, this vast region, because of this solar energy wealth and by applying technologies already available, could become the energy source for its own use and by high voltage networks supply much of Europe and India. Western United States, Australia, Southwest Africa, Kazakhstan, Western China, and Chile also have similar high solar energy potential.

Wind Power. Windmills were mentioned as an early use of natural energy sources. For centuries wind power has been used to propel ships, pump water and grind grain. Dutch windmills to drain the below sea level polders are a common feature in our memories. Standard features in the farm landscape of the United States in decades past were tall-standing windmills to pump water for home use and livestock. However, like solar power, wind power is not available everywhere all the time. Sometimes there is no wind, and in many places the wind is rarely strong enough or persistent enough to make it a dependable source of power.

Even so, in recent decades isolated electricity generating windmills and "windmill farms" are springing up across the land in places where average winds are dependable and strong enough. Most electricity generating windmills are very tall with three long blades that turn slowly. Individual windmills might provide power for a farm owner, with some power left over to sell to a local utility.

A single windmill in a good location can produce enough power for 150 to 400 homes. Utility owned "windmill farms" produce power for one or more communities.

Denmark is the world's number one nation in terms of use of wind power to produce energy (about 30% of their total energy use). Denmark also is number one in the world in manufacturing wind power machines, producing about 40% of all wind machines in the world market. This small country by the North Sea also has several offshore "windmill farms" where full advantage of wind power is possible without interference from features on the land.

As with solar power, wind generator development has not reached its peak. Already there are other types of wind machines, including a vertical type with blades like an egg beater and one called a "Wind Amplified Rotor Platform" (WARP) that has layers of cups on a center post that trap winds and spin. Electricity generation by solar power and wind have tremendous advantages over most other energy sources: They create no air pollution, they depend on natural sources of energy, no fossil fuels are consumed, and they cause no health problems! There is concern, however, that the tips of long blades moving at high speed do kill birds.

Geothermal. Geothermal energy has been important for centuries in some ancient volcano areas. It is well known that a few thousand feet below the surface the temperature is extremely hot. Since Iceland's settlement, steam emanating from the ground has been used for bathing and washing. From the late 1700s when wells were first sunk, more and more of Iceland's buildings and homes have been heated and provided with electricity generated from steam from deep sources. Northern Italy and New Zealand also have been among the early users of geothermal steam energy.

Technologies developed in the last few decades also are using the constancy of moderate temperatures below the Earth's surface for heating and cooling homes and other buildings using geothermal principles. Pipes drilled dozens or a few hundred feet below buildings circulate a refrigerant that, like a heat pump operating in the air, can keep a building warm in winter and cool in summer using electrical energy only to operate the pumps and air circulation system in the building. Based on the constancy of the temperature below the surface, the deep piping is much more efficient and less costly than surface heat pumps.

The "geothermal principle" was recently used in the construction of two buildings in Carbondale, Illinois. One is on the campus of Southern Illinois University, the other building is the Center for Independent Living. These systems require very little maintenance, and experience shows that the system will pay for itself in about five years. They do require a dependable source of electricity to operate the pumps.

There is encouraging geothermal research and development underway involving other geothermal energy sources that are a few thousand feet below the surface. These include coalbed methane, deep natural gas, and methane hydrates, all with listings on the Internet. However, as encouraging as this research is, again we should not plan our energy future on the basis of technologies that are not ready to be applied on scales that will make a significant difference in our increasing global energy demand.

Final Point. As available technologies now stand, applying available wind, biomass and solar technologies cannot provide enough energy to fulfill—in time—the ever-increasing global demand that is happening, so it is not surprising that new nuclear power plants are being built in many place, especially in Europe.

APPENDIX D: IDEAS AND ETHICS THAT MATTER

<u>D1: Seven common religious beliefs agreed upon by religious leaders at the 1970 organizing meeting of the "World Conference of Religions for Peace":</u>

1. An acknowledgment of the fundamental unity of the human family, of the equality and dignity of all human beings.

2. A sense of the sacredness of the individual person and his/her conscience.

3. A sense of the value of the human community.

4. A recognition that "might" is not right, that human power is not self-sufficient and absolute.

5. A belief that love, compassion, unselfishness and the force of inner truthfulness and of the spirit ultimately have greater power that hate, enmity and self interest.

6. A sense of obligation to stand on the side of the poor and the oppressed and against the rich and the oppressors.

7. A profound hope that good will finally prevail.

D2: "Declaration of a Global Ethic", seven points agreed upon at Second Parliament of World Religions, Chicago, 1993:

1. We are interdependent. Each of us depends on the well-being of the whole, and so we must have respect for the community of living beings, for people, animals, and plants, and for the preservation of Earth, the air, water and soil.

2. We must take individual responsibility for all we do. All our decisions, actions, and failures to act have consequences.

3. We must treat others as we wish others to treat us. We make a commitment to respect life and dignity, individuality and diversity, so that every person is treated humanely, without exception.

4. We consider humankind to be our family. We must strive to be kind and generous. We must not live for ourselves alone, but should also serve others, never forgetting the children, the aged, the poor, the suffering, the disabled, the refugees and the lonely.

5. We commit ourselves to a culture of non-violence, respect, justice and peace.

6. We must strive for a just social and economic order, in which everyone has an equal chance to reach full potential as a human being. We must move beyond the dominance of greed for power, prestige, money and consumption to make a just and peaceful world.

7. Earth cannot be changed for the better unless the consciousness of individuals is changed first. Therefore we commit ourselves to the global ethic, to understanding one another, and to socially-beneficial, peace-fostering, and nature-friendly ways of life.

D3. Six Ethical Points for the Future, from *2005 State of the Future*, page 6.

1. Harmony with nature is more important than economic progress.

2. Protection of the environment and biodiversity should be considered in any policy.

3. The rights of women and children are uninfringeable and fundamental for a healthy society.

4. World interests should prevail over nation-state interests.

5. Human space migration is part of human evolution.

6. Any artificial form of life intelligent enough to request rights should be given these rights and be treated with the same respect as humans. (I assume this refers to living results of stem cell research, not to robots.)

APPENDIX E: "ESPERANTO" AS A SECOND LANGUAGE

"Esperanto" was invented by L. L. Zamenhof of Poland in the 1880s. It was presented to the world as a workable and easy to learn "second language" and is based on Romance (Latin), Germanic and Slavic language word roots and sounds. Esperanto is viewed as an appropriate international language in part because of its "neutrality". It has not been adopted officially by any country but is used in many international venues. Although English speaking is on the rise around the world and is rich in its flexibility, it is a complicated, is difficult to learn, and carries much "cultural baggage" from its European origin.

Adoption of Esperanto as the official language of a new Limited Global Government would simplify all of its operations (Global Parliament, Global Peace/Police Force, and Executive staff). Personnel would be drawn from all parts of the world to staff the Global Government, and having a common language would facilitate recruitment and all operations and keep one language (English) and culture from dominating.

BIBLIOGRAPHY AND SELECTED REFERENCES

INTRODUCTION

Brown, Lester R., *Plan B 2.0*, W.W. Norton & Co., New York, 2006.

Christensen, David E., *Healing the World*, iUniverse, New York, 2005

Clayton, Mark, "Life on Tired Earth", *Christian Science Monitor*, Apr. 1, 2005, <http://www.alternet.org/envirohealth.21645/>.

Diamond, Jared, *Guns, Germs and Steel*, W.W. Norton & Co., New York, 1999.

Ehrlich, Paul, *The Population Bomb*, Balantine, New York, 1968.

Ehrlich, Paul and Anne, *The Population Explosion*, Touchstone, New York, 1990.

Glenn, Jerome C. and Gordon, Theodore J., *2005 State of the Future*. [Accompanied by a 3500 page CD and Executive Summary, developed through the American Council for The United Nations University, as part of the UN Millennium Project.]

Gore, Al, *An Inconvenient Truth*, Rodale Books, Emmaus, PA, 2006.

Hukill, Tracy, a report of the "UN Millennium Ecosystem Assessment" presented on the Internet: <http://www.alternet.org.story/31222/>.

Kunstler, James H., The Long Emergency, Atlantic Monthly Press, New York, 2005.

Maddox, John, *The Doomsday Syndrome*, McGraw Hill, New York, 1972.

Sachs, Jeffrey D., *The End of Poverty*, Penguin, London, 2005.

Soyinka, Wole, *Climate of Fear*, Random House, New York, 2004.

Wilson, Edward O., *Consilience*, Alfred Knopf, New York, 1998.

World Bank, *The Little Green Data Book 06*, World Bank, Washington, D.C., 1906, [Includes a wide range of data on world regions and all nations.]

World Resources Institute, *Ecosystems and Human Well-Being*, A report of the Millennium Ecosystem Assessment, Island Press, Washington, D.C., 2005.

PART A: BASICS OF SURVIVAL—Planet Earth and the Evolution of Life

Bryant, Peter J., *Biodiversity and Conservation*, Chapter 2, "Ancient Life (Paleozoic) 600-230 M.Y.B.P.", <http://www.dbc.uci.edu/~sustain/bio65/lec02/b65lec02.htm>.

Hickman, Martin, "Earth's Ecological Debt Crisis: Mankind's 'Borrowing' from Nature Hits New Record", Common Dreams News Center, Oct. 9, 2006, <http://www.commondreams.org/headlines06/1009-o3.htm>.

Palmer, A.R., "Evaluating Ecological Footprints", *Electronic Green Journal*, December 1998, Special Issue 9, <http://egj.lib.uidaho.edu/egj09/palmer1.html>.

Chapter 1: Atmosphere—Oxygen

Conner, Steve, "Ice Bubbles Reveal Biggest Rise in CO2 for 800,000 Years", Common Dreams News Center, Sept. 5, 2006, <http://www.common-dreams.org/headlines06/0905-06.htm>.

Gore, op. cit.

Milliken, Mary, "World has 10-Year Window to Act on Climate Warming—NASA Expert", Common Dreams News Center, Sept. 14, 2006, <http://www.commondreams.org/headlines06/0914-01.htm>.

Monbiot, George, "Mocking Our Dreams", *The Guardian*, Feb. 5, 2005, <http://www.guardian.co.uk/comment/story/0,3604,1414660,00.html>.

Parmesan, Camille, *Audubon*, Sept.-Oct. 2005.

Chapter 2: Fresh Water

Bair, Julene, "Turn Off the Spigots", AlterNet, June 14, 2005, <http://www.alternet.org/envirohealth/22229/>.

Beck, Juliette, "Building a Water Democracy", AlterNet, June 1, 2005, <http://www.alternet.org/envirohealth/22144/>.

Brown, Lester R., op. cit., Chapter 3, "Emerging Water Shortages", pp. 41-58.

Internet item on coral reefs <http://www.washingtonpost.com/wp-dyn/content/article/2006/07/04/AR2006070400772_pf>.

Roy, Arundhati, *Power Politics*, South End Press, Cambridge, MA, 2002.

Sachs, Jeffrey, "War Climates", Tom Paine Common Sense, Oct. 23, 2006, <http://www.tompaine.com/print/war_climates.php>.

Sengupta, Somini, "India Digs Deeper, but Wells Are Drying Up", *New York Times*, Sept. 30, 2006, <http://www.nytimes.com/2006/09/30/world/asia/30water2.html>.

Shiva, Vandana, *Water Wars*, South End Press, Cambridge, MA, 2002.

Simon, Paul, *Tapped Out*, Welcome Rain, New York, 2002.

Specter, Michael, "The Last Drop", *The New Yorker*, Oct. 23, 2006, pp. 60-71.

Chapter 3: Food and Fiber

Committee for the National Institute for the Environment, "Population and Arable Land", <http://www.cnie.org/pop/conserving//landuse2b.htm>.

FAO (Food and Agricultural Organization-U.N.), *Dimensions of Need—An Atlas of Food and Agriculture*, FAO Corporate Document Repository, 1995, ISBN 92-5-103737-X, <http://www.fao.org//docrep/u8480e/u8480e0e.htm>.

George, Susan, *Feeding the Few: Corporate Control of Food*, Institute for Policy Studies, Washington, D.C., 1979.

Gore, op. cit.

Internet: "GeographyIQ", <http://www.geographyiq.com/ranking/ranking_Land_Use_Arable_land_dall.htm>.

Larsen, Janet, "Population Growth Leading to Land Hunger", Earth Policy Institute, Jan. 23, 2003-1, <http://www.earth-policy.org/Updates/Updates21_printable.htm>.

Manning, Richard, "The Oil We Eat: Following the Food Chain Back to Iraq", *Harper's*, Feb. 2004, <http://www.harpers.org/TheOilWeEat.html>.

Meadows, Donella H. and others, *The Limits to Growth*, Universe Books, 1972.

National Geographic Society, *A World Transformed*, a map published in 2002.

Pimentel, David and Mario Giampietro, "Food, Land, Population and the U.S. Economy", Carrying Capacity Network, 2000 P Street, N.W., Suite 240, Washington, D.C., 1994.

Pimentel, David and Marcia Pimental, "Land, Energy and Water: The Constraints Governing Ideal U.S. Population Size", NPG FORUM, reprinted in *CNN Focus*, Spring 1991, <http://dieoff.org/page136.htm>.

Population Action International, "III. Population and Arable Land", Conserving Land, Population and /Sustainable Food Production, ca 1994, <http://www.cnie.org/pop/conserving/landuse2b.htm>.

Smith, J. W., "The World's Wasted Wealth", a twenty page 1994 monograph, Internet,<http://www.ied.info/books/www.feedingtheworld.html>.

USGS, "Assessing the Impact of Urban Sprawl on Soil Resources in the United States Using Nighttime 'City Lights', Satellite Images and Digital Soils Maps", by Marc Imhoss and others, <http://biology.usgs.gov/luhna/chap3.html>.

Chapter 4: Building Materials

Chapter 5: Energy—"Energy Slaves"

Internet, Earth Policy news item (on Swedish shift tax): <Earthpolicynews@ earthpolicy.org, Plan B Book Byte 2006-4, April 12, 2006>.

Hightower, Jim, "Mountain Top Removal", *The Hightower Lowdown*, Nov. 2005 issue.

Internet, for more information on the Supreme Court recording error that gave personhood to U.S. corporations: <http://www.alternet.org/ module/printversion/38406>.

Kunstler, James H., op. cit.

Manning, Richard, op. cit.

Mitchell, John G., "The Coal Paradox", *National Geographic*, March 2006, pp, 98-123.

Voices for Creative Nonviolence, Chicago, full report on Production Sharing Agreements available on the Internet at: <www.crudedesigns.org>.

PART B: WHAT MAKES US "DIFFERENT"?—People and Culture
Chapter 6: Education

Blake, Rev. J. L., *Geography for Children*, Richardson, Lord and Holbrook, Boston, 1831.

Colton, *Colton's New Introductory Geography*, Sheldon & Co., New York, 1875.

Douglas, William O., *Points of Rebellion*, Vantage, New York, 1970.

Higbee, Edward, *The Squeeze: Cities Without Space*, Morrow, New York, 1960.

Internet, Robert Hutchins quotes.

Joyce, Frank, "Cuban Exiles Wage War of Terror", AlterNet, August 16, 2006, <http://www.org/module/printversion/40370>.

Loewen, James W., *Lies My Teacher Told Me*, Touchstone, New York, 1995.

Tuchman, Barbara, *The March of Folly: From Troy to Vietnam*, Alfred Knopf, New York, 1984.

Zinn, Howard, *A People's History of the United States: 1492 to Present*, Harper Perennial, New York, 1995.

Chapter 7: Religion (and The Arts)

Barrows, Rev. John Henry (Ed.), *The World's Parliament of Religions* (2 volumes), The Parliament Publishing Company, Chicago, 1893.

Ehrman, Bart C., *Misquoting Jesus*, Harper, San Francisco, 2005.

Kidder, Tracy, *Mountains beyond Mountains*, Random House, New York, 2004.

Kjos, Berit, "Gorbachev's Plan for a United World", Internet: <http://www.crossroad.to/text/articles/gorb 10-95.html>.

Oughton, David Charles, *The Implications of Henry Nelson Wieman's Philosophy of Creative Interchange for World Peace*, unpublished dissertation presented to faculty of Graduate School of Saint Louis University, 1998.

Stone, Merlin, *When God Was A Woman*, Dorset, New York, 1976.

Vonnegut, Kurt, "Cold Turkey", June 7, 2004, Internet: Alternet.org.

Wieman, Henry Nelson, *Religious Inquiry, Some Explorations*, Beacon Press, Boston, 1969

Wieman, *The Source of Human Good*, Southern Illinois University Press, Carbondale, 1946.

Chapter 8: Law and "Limited World Government"

Deudney, Daniel, *Whole Earth Security: A Geopolitics of Peace*, Worldwatch Paper 55, Worldwatch Institute, Washington, D.C., 1983.

Douglas, op. cit.

Goff, Stan, "American Fascism Is on the Rise", AlterNet, Oct. 14, 2006, <http://www.alternet.org/module/printversion/42884>.

Higbee, Edward, *A Question of Priorities*, Morrow, New York, 1970.

Joyce, Frank, "Cuban Exiles Wage War of Terror", AlterNet, Aug. 16, 2006, <http://www.aslternat.org/module/printversion/40370>.

Kjos, op. cit.

Reves, Emery, *The Anatomy of Peace*, Harper and Brothers, New York, 1945.

Tuchman, Barbara, op. cit.

PART C: OUR FUTURE IS UP TO US!
Chapter 9: Summary of Parts A and B

Brown, Lester, *The Twenty-Ninth Day*, Norton, New York, 1978.

Burch, Guy I. and Pendell, Elmer, *Human Breeding and Survival*, Penguin Books, New York, 1945.

Lyford, Joseph, "Vote for World Peace", *New Republic*, 12-27-48, pp. 16-18.

Stepanek, Mattie, *Just Peace*, Andrews McMeel Publishing, Kansas City, 2006.

Chapter 10: Coping With Overpopulation

Brown, Lester R., "U.S. Population Reaches 300 Million, Heading for 400 Million, No Cause for Celebration", *Earth Policy N ews,* Oct. 4, 2006, <http://www.earthpolicy.org/Updates/2006/Update59.htm>.

Burch, Guy Irving and Pendell, Elmer, op.cit.

Czeck, Brian, *Shoveling Fuel for a Runaway Train*, Univ. of California Press, Berkeley, 2000.

Ehrlich, Paul R., *The Population Bomb*, Ballantine, New York, 1968.

Maury, Marian (Ed.), *Birth Rate and Birth Rite*, McFadden, New York, 1963.

Menken, Jane (Ed.), *World Population and U.S. Policy*, Norton, New York, 1986.

Peter, Laurence J., *The Peter Plan, A Proposal for Survival*, William Morrow, New York, 1976.

Sauvy, Alfred, *Fertility and Survival*, Collier, New York, 1963.

Wilson, op. cit., p. 255.

Chapter 11: Conclusion and Challenge

Barney, Gerald O., *Threshold 2000, Critical Issues and Spiritual Values for a Global Age*, CoNexus Press, Ada, MI, 1999. (Prepared for 1999 Parliament of World Religions, Cape Town, South Africa.

Czeck, Brian, op. cit.

Korten, David C., *The Great Turning*, Barrett-Koehler, San Francisco, 2006.

Peter, Laurence J., op. cit.

Stone, Merlin, *When God Was a Woman*, Dorset, New York, 1976.

EPILOGUE

Czeck, Brian, op. cit.

Diamond, Jared, *Guns, Germs, and Steel*, Norton, New York, 1997.

Duffy, James, *Shipwreck and Empire*, Harvard University Press, Cambridge, 1955.

Eisler, Riane, *The Chalice and the Blade*, Harper, San Francisco, 1987.

Korten, op. cit.

McKibbon, Bill, "How Close a Catastrophe?", AlterNet, Nov. 4, 2006, <http://www.alternet.org/module/printversion/43606>.

Sachs, Jeffrey D., *The End of Poverty,* Penguin, New York, 2005.

Stone, Merlin, op. cit.

INDEX

978-0-595-42427-6
0-595-42427-9